Critical Guides to French Texts

111 Sartre: Huis clos *and* Les Séquestrés d'Altona

Critical Guides to French Texts

EDITED BY ROGER LITTLE, WOLFGANG VAN EMDEN, DAVID WILLIAMS

SARTRE

Huis clos
and
Les Séquestrés d'Altona

Walter Redfern

Professor in the Department of French Studies
University of Reading

Grant & Cutler Ltd
1995

© Grant & Cutler Ltd
1995
ISBN 0 7293 0383 7

DEPÓSITO LEGAL: V. 4.793 - 1995

Printed in Spain by
Artes Gráficas Soler, S.A., Valencia
for
GRANT & CUTLER LTD
55-57 GREAT MARLBOROUGH STREET, LONDON W1V 2AY

Contents

Prefatory Note	7
1. Sartre on Theatre	9
2. *Huis clos*	13
3. Bridge Passage	33
4. *Les Séquestrés d'Altona*	35
Bibliography	80

Prefatory Note

The editions used for both plays are 'Folio', Gallimard. References, in the style *5*, p.128, are to numbered entries in the Bibliography. *Huis clos* is abbreviated as *HC* and *Les Séquestrés d'Altona* as *SA*.

1. Sartre on Theatre

True to his preference for thumbscrew theatre, Sartre installs torture at the anguished core of both *Huis clos* and *Les Séquestrés d'Altona*. 'Question' in French covers in English the possibly neutral 'question', the intimidating 'interrogation', and the explicit 'torture'. The harsh light of the third-degree burns unrelentingly on Sartre's stage. Both plays are animated by death: ex-mortals in *Huis clos*, the living dead in *Les Séquestrés d'Altona*. Both revolve around guilt and bad faith. The first takes place in a closed room, the second in a twin sets of rooms. Behind shut doors, but before our very eyes, each play puts its protagonists on trial.

Though there are numerous constants in Sartre's theatre, I want to avoid suggesting that his beliefs and practices were static. They did evolve, and he often contradicted himself. One of his most lasting credos was that 'le théâtre est philosophique et la philosophie est dramatique'.[1] In 1960, Sartre roundly condemned much contemporary theatre as strictly insane, 'parce qu'on a choisi de couper la tête à tous ces personnages, de leur ôter la liberté [...] de leur ôter les projets' (5, p.126). Although this criticism could be turned back against his own practice in the two plays studied, where he largely deprives his characters of freedom of manoeuvre, their desperate debates on their plights are the stuff of intense drama. They have, if no other, freedom of speech. Sixteen years earlier, Sartre was already focusing on theatre as a conflict of rights (a pet theme for the litigious French), and pointing to Corneille as the great precursor here (5, pp.30, 59). In this view, theatre involves power-struggles, and so is inherently political.

---

[1] Sartre, in interview with Madeleine Chapsal, *Les Ecrivains en personne* (Julliard, 1960), p.208.

In distinguishing plays from fiction, Sartre assumes that theatrical space itself, the physical separation of audience from the stage, sets up an inevitable distance, but also promotes direct experience of the spectacle. The audience sees with its own eyes, not via the agency of the novelist's words (*5*, pp.22-25). Would-be 'real-life' props are of moderate concern to Sartre. He works always towards the general, which he often calls 'myth'. By this he means not only classical mythology, but also general themes that move beyond the individual. Such 'myth' depends for its staging on conscious artifice. In all this, however, the stress on distancing is meant to persuade spectators to recognize themselves, at a remove, in the stage personages, their dramatic situation and their physical context.

It would be a splendid instance of what Sartre in *Critique de la raison dialectique* calls 'contre-finalité' (unintended result) that *Huis clos*, Sartre's most contrived play (talking corpses in Hell), bites as hard as any other play of his, if he had not willed this paradox by his constant insistence on the dramatic necessity of distancing, ritual and myth. His strategy is to defamiliarize a theme as a prelude to ramming it down our throats. His major enemy was always the atomization of the twentieth-century theatre audience. Though he made adroit use of the self-referential potentiality of the theatre – the dramatic irony of the actress playing Inès ordering fellow actors to stop play-acting: 'Ne jouez pas cette comédie' (*HC*, p.49) – he was not very interested in scenic innovation for its own sake. If he at times went out on a limb, as in the infernal setting of *Huis clos*, the excursion was always firmly wedded to his pointed demonstration of argument.

Sartre's principal theatrical renovation derives from a central tenet of Existentialism: 'L'homme n'est pas une nature, c'est un drame: ses caractères sont des actes' (*3 (1)*, p.150). Human reality is not congealed into an unchanging character or essence. 'Ce que le théâtre peut montrer de plus émouvant est un caractère en train de se faire, le moment du choix, de la libre décision qui engage une morale et toute une vie' (*5*, p.20). Character is thus an incremental process, ending only at death. The corpses of *Huis clos* have clearly missed their opportunity for such self-creation while alive; their agony lies in their gradual realization of the awful wastage. Despite his broadsides against 'character' as a theatrical convention, in his plays as in his fiction, Sartre could or would not forgo some elements of character in the normal sense: temperament, idiosyncrasy, if only to make the figments interesting and distinguishable from each other. Self-creation needs some built-in repetition.

Another obstacle in the path of evolving character is the wilfully stereotyped nature of the three protagonists in *Huis clos*: macho male, superficial socialite, and bitchy lesbian. They furnish a perverse proof that theatre, like life, lies if it lays claim to fixity of nature. This trio, among other things, are played-out theatrical types wishing vainly to be authentic humans. They condemn themselves to enact a parody of love's roundabout and undergo the macabre ordeal of death-in-life. Such banality also helps to bring philosophy down to earth from the clouds. Sharing in the national sport of many writers over the past two centuries, Sartre does the dirty on his class of origin. He does this because for him people are stereotypes, social caricatures, unless they take themselves in hand and make free choices. Sartre was often surprisingly unhostile to middlebrow bourgeois theatre (and most of his plays were in fact put on in such establishments). He was always fully prepared to use ready-made theatrical sorcery for his own different goal of effecting a 'mental mutation' in his spectators (5, p.175).

'Character' is, of course, a slippery concept. Despite what the trio of *Huis clos* claim, none of them had in their life on earth a fixed character; each was free to choose differently. Only once dead do they take on an unchangeable essence, for Sartre a kind of living death. Any alteration they experience in Hell is one of the stripping away of lies. The whole play, psychologically, moves in reverse: they unmake themselves and each other; they are reduced to their truth. For many a year, Sartre found Freud's theories, in which the subconscious determines actions, too permissive, too fatalistic, too exempt of willpower. Sartre's villains are Freudians, their author not.

For Sartre, freedom, the bedrock of Existentialism, is a kind of original sin that we are all born with. We are cursed with this precious gift, condemned to be free (*1*, p.639). We seek to escape the challenge of this bracing imposition by retreating into bad faith. We are thus not so much human-all-too-human as not-yet-human. We will never be fully human until we face up to the challenge of our freedom, a birthright we so regularly squander. In this view, we will our weaknesses, and indeed spend enormous energy in such self-defeating misapplications. In this theory of our total responsibility for ourselves, Sartre can sound hopelessly idealistic and demanding. When, however, he shifts from individuals to their fellows and their contexts, he reintroduces less deniable facts of life: 'Chaque situation est une souricière, des murs partout' (*3 (2)*, p.313). Our room for manoeuvre is severely hampered by the presence and competing claims of other individuals. We cannot act in a void. The original title of *Huis clos* was *Les Autres*.

2. *Huis clos*

Occupied Paris, late May 1944: air-raid sirens, power failures, rationing, curfews, and a suffocating atmosphere of inescapable surveillance. The first performance of *Huis clos* antedated the Normandy landings by just over a week (27 May). The knee-jerk reaction by moral majoritarian reviewers was that the play exhibited decadent immorality (the play was banned in England in 1946 by the Lord Chamberlain, because it included lesbianism). France was just emerging from the trauma of Occupation, amid much searching of hearts and consciences over questions of guilt and responsibility, especially that of collaboration with the enemy. The idea of *Huis clos* stemmed from a suggestion by Marc Barbezat for a play designed for his wife Olga and for Wanda Kosakiewicz, which could easily be taken on tour: short, a single set, and 2-3 characters. Sartre was tempted. His first image was of people trapped in a cellar during a bombing-raid. He invited Camus to direct and act the part of Garcin, but after some rehearsals Camus withdrew. In 1968, Sartre recalled his prison-camp experience of living under constant surveillance. He stressed also that he wanted all the actors to have parts of equal weight. He therefore ensured that they all remained on stage, after their introduction, throughout. He could naturally have opted for a different setting, for example a group of prisoners on death-row, going over their past lives. *Huis clos* extends the old commonplace that a drowning person sees the whole of his or her previous existence passing before the eyes.

The period of the Occupation was commonly known as 'la période en vase clos': in isolation. This is the situation of Garcin, Inès and Estelle. The term 'huis clos' is the French legal equivalent of 'in camera' (behind closed doors) in English. The play is also translated as *No Exit*. *Huis clos* could also be a pun on 'huit clos': the mathematical symbol for infinity, suitable for the eternity of

Hell. There is no way out of an 8. It is a vicious circle or circuit, a Catch-22 situation. As for its original title, *Les Autres*, this is a play not focused, like so many, on a central hero or heroine, but on a group. A play based on interaction, which can be, if not invariably, the very heart of drama. Each of the three parties is a third party to the other two at some point.

Though the fourth wall is absent, thus enabling the audience to pry into the lives on display, a theatre is itself *à huis clos*. The spectators are closed in, for a space of time; the actors' parts tie them to the stage. All arts implicitly ask us to accept their artifice, their special conventions. In *Huis clos*, we are requested to admit that three corpses can still function, after a fashion. They can face up to their past life, or try to run away from it on the spot, even if they no longer have any future, nor indeed any possibility of truthfully rewriting the script of their biography. They are left, then, with attitude and style. What do they make of their lives, in two senses? What did they do with them; and how do they interpret what they did? Within the confines of their hell-hole, the three can still talk, gesture, move about, but otherwise they are stalled, trapped, damned. Like people in prisons, air-raid shelters, hospitals or steerage, they have to live (so to speak) in compulsory cohabitation. Although Sartre sets them at the greatest possible distance from us (they are dead, we alive), he wants us to feel a guilty kinship with them, as a prelude to judging them, and ourselves. As with the moral terrorism of the Christian apologist and forerunner of Existentialism, Pascal, *Huis clos* is intended to frighten us with a cautionary tale. By showing us starkly where a rejection of personal freedom leads, Sartre hopes to startle us into living more authentically. The abolition of a future is the cruellest fate imaginable for an Existentialist, whose philosophy is forward-directed. Sartre coined the term 'inexistentialisme' to typify the trio's refusal of their freedom (*4*, p.100).

Sartre's self-imposed task here is to convey the terrible infinity of suffering (they are there till Hell ices over) in one and a half hours. He achieves this chiefly by pulling the threads of interpersonal conflict ever tighter so that, ultimately, there remains truly no escape. Hell is of course in this play also a formal device, a way, as with myth, of distancing events the better to focus on them, as in longsightedness. Nothing could be further from, or nearer to, the living than death. Moreover, like many atheists, Sartre needs the idea of Hell, even if he adapts it for his own purposes, in order to embody the active presence of evil and its consequences in human affairs. He can manage without Heaven. Bad faith in Existentialism matches the Christian concept of Original Sin. In both cases, we give in to temptations, seeking easy ways out, self-gratification, or evasion of duties. Of traditional Hell Sartre retains only the heat, but of more bearable intensity. His three people are hell-bent, anyway, on putting each other in the hot spot; they grill each other. Sartre in fact switches to an emphasis on mutual mental torture. Its exquisitely sadistic potential renders fiery furnaces and prancing demons with pitchforks superfluous. The three give each other hell.

The movement of this drama goes from total lies to part-lies to the truth. It is a stripping process, caught exactly in the image of them 'naked as worms' (p.52). In this process, to counteract solipsism – talking to or seeing only yourself – others play a crucial role. They develop us, as if we were negatives waiting to be exposed. They are indispensable, and yet intolerable, necessary and dangerous to us. The Other seeks to dominate the I, but at the same time forces that I, that eye, to open to the truth. We need others, then, to define us, to define ourselves against. If, however, we sign away too much of our own initiative, we become an object in others' eyes, and thus a fake subject. In this way, other people, like all aspects of human reality for Sartre, are ambivalent. They can back up, or destabilize. Though this is probably wishful thinking, we should not yield to their domination, nor subject them to ours. Sartre believed that in practice a master/slave relationship usually prevails.

Commenting in a spoken foreword to a recording of *Huis clos* on the notorious formula 'L'enfer, c'est les autres', Sartre explained: 'Si les rapports avec autrui sont tordus, viciés, alors l'autre ne peut être que l'enfer'. Above all, he stressed that 'quel que soit le cercle d'enfer dans lequel nous vivons, je pense que nous sommes libres de le briser. Et si les gens ne le brisent pas, c'est encore librement qu'ils y restent. De sorte qu'ils se mettent librement en enfer' (*4*, pp.101-02). No role, then, for the despatch-clerk St Peter at the pearly gates. If 'hell is other people' and the final line 'Eh bien, continuons' seem gloomy, they are so as regards these three people. A different script would be needed for protagonists who forced themselves to act honestly and courageously. In addition, if each of us is condemned to be free, and each is an Other to another, we are equivalent to everybody else, and so Hell is ourselves also. In other words, the phrase was intended by Sartre not as a misanthropic generalization and bromide, but as a goad, a dose of salts, a trampoline towards reflection and effort to change. Not the last word, but the first: a basis for alternative action. It is a terrorist play, aimed at putting the fear of God into us, so that we avoid the inauthentic choices of the three damned souls.

In biographical terms, the trio partly derives from that of Sartre, Simone de Beauvoir and Olga Kosakiewicz. The failure of their tripartite experimental liaison foreshadowed the three-way tugs of *Huis clos*, which exploits the Eternal Triangle at a pitch of intensity undreamt of by Mills and Boon. Each character in the play was already caught up in triangles on earth: Estelle/her husband/her lover; Inès/Florence/Florence's husband (Inès's cousin); Garcin/his wife/his mistress. Two is company, three's a crowd. The third party is, in the Italian term, *un terzo incomodo*, a gooseberry, like a duenna. Though history shows the unreliability of such treaties, in which temporary neutrality camouflages hostile longer-term plans, Garcin offers a mutual non-aggression pact. Both Inès and he, however, realize that they all represent traps for each other. In his words, 'Nous nous courrons après comme des chevaux de bois, sans jamais nous rejoindre' (p.66). The carrousel of feigned or unavailing love, and of only too palpable enmity. Each will end up wanting, impossibly, to flee the others; or, in a comic twist, Estelle and Garcin will gang up to wrestle with Inès in order to eject this unwelcome intruder (p.87). Whereas both Garcin and Inès expect to be punished, though in his case for lesser misdemeanours than his actual crimes, Estelle persists in claiming exemption on the grounds of innocence. She covers up quickly after her initial mistaking of Garcin with his head in his hands for her earthly lover with his face blown away in the suicide she provoked (p.27). Eventually, all three come to state truthfully the manner of their dying, though each delays confessing the true reasons. They share, then, a common situation, but each varies in his or her strategies of denial and manoeuvring of others.

Garcin

With a characteristic mixture of mild self-criticism and blatant pride, Garcin admits early on: 'Je vivais toujours dans des meubles que je n'aimais pas et des situations fausses; j'adorais ça' (p.14). He will not seriously lacerate himself ('j'ai l'habitude de me taquiner' (p.18) – a merely epidermic needling). Perverseness indeed typifies his behaviour and thinking. Despite his refrain – 'Je veux regarder la situation en face' (p.17) – he buries his head, ostrich-fashion, in his hands. In Hell there is no such privacy. Although he acknowledges that they will all be eventually stripped to the bone, in such concealment he clearly exhibits shame. For Sartre, shame results from feeling that your existence is unjustified, and in *L'Etre et le Néant* he alludes to the shame of the denuded Adam and Eve. Though Garcin's life has been terminated, he talks as if it were still in the making: 'Il faut que je mette ma vie en ordre' (p.25). Throughout the play, he oscillates between throwing in the towel and bouts of aggressiveness. As well as self-imposed silence, he looks, like the worldly Estelle, to politeness as a buffer-zone against contagious hostility.

    He lived in Rio de Janeiro and, by contamination, suffers from machismo. Recalling his newspaper office, he fondly evokes men in shirtsleeves, male flesh and cigar fug. In Hell he still wants, fruitlessly, to impress, indeed to seduce, men, just as Inès desires to worship, hurt and subordinate women. His male vanity dictates the initial version of his story. As a pacifist journalist, he refused to join up when war broke out, and was executed: a noble death for a just cause. Until late on in the drama, he will admit only so much, for example that he maltreated his wife. He presents her, besides, as a born victim, accident-prone, a martyr -- whereas he himself will be revealed as refusing martyrdom for his professed cause of pacifism. It costs him little to confess to abusing his wife, as this chimes in with his self-image as 'un dur'. In his account, she brought his sadism on herself. On earth already, then, he was practising mental cruelty, when he installed his mulatto mistress in the conjugal bed and obliged his wife to serve them breakfast (p.54). He later reports, with casual callousness, her death from a broken heart (p.81).

In many ways, this bourgeois intellectual (as the French consider upmarket journalists) and would-be macho is the feeblest of the three. He is the only one who hopes to salvage himself from the wreckage, as if change were still an option, whereas Inès admits she is justly condemned, and Estelle can recognize her actions, without ostensibly being much shaken in recalling them. Garcin holds a stereotypically masculine, confrontational view of their 'hosts' as 'ils': malicious beings conspiring to set traps. For him, the situation of the three in Hell is a contest of wills against their aggressors. Despite his parasitic dependence on men's approval, when he finally resees his former office, he resists the evidence of insults to his memory that he overhears (p.76). When he at last utters his true confession, that he died badly, as a coward in flight, he does so grudgingly, and qualifies it as always by attempts at self-justification (pp.78-79). *Comédie* is a key concept in the play, and *hypocrite* has the root-meaning 'stage-actor'. Much of the time, Garcin is a ham, posturing and unconvincing.

He is not, as Inès and Estelle are, forgotten by his survivors, but such remembrance adds to his torment. He is obsessed with the relay-race of condemnatory recollection. 'Ils mourront, mais d'autres viendront, qui prendront la consigne: je leur ai laissé ma vie entre les mains'. He is, he adds, 'Fait comme un rat [...] Je suis tombé dans le domaine public' (p.82). Obviously, when dead we no longer have any control over what others think of us; we lose our own copyright in ourselves. If the living cannot help the dead, perhaps a fellow *morte vivante*, Estelle, may. If, one in a thousand, she refuses to label him definitively as a coward, he will be 'saved'. Like Estelle, he regrets the absence of a mirror in the room thoughtfully furnished for them, because he too depends far too much on others' opinions of him (Sartre's term for this: 'être-pour-autrui'). He wants a human mirror to reflect back to him his self-estimate. This would of course be a magic mirror, telling him he is the fairest of them all. The pathetic attempt at 'un délire à deux', a twin madness (recycled in *Les Séquestrés d'Altona* between Frantz and Johanna), relies on Estelle's promise that, as she could not love a coward, and she needs to focus on him, he cannot therefore be a coward (p.83). This is plainly illogical, and illustrates Sartre's special use of the word 'emotion' to signify would-be 'magical' reasoning, wish-fulfilment. Like worry beads or blankets, such tactics seek to console, to ward off unpleasant reality. Similarly, Garcin's fits of temper, his urges to strike out, represent a 'magical' flight from a situation he will not honestly face.

When, however, he grows disgusted with both women, and tries physically to escape by hammering on the door, he rejects Estelle's advances. He takes refuge, instead, in the Sartrian stereotype of woman as a soft, sticky trap: 'Tu est moite! tu es molle! Tu es une pieuvre, tu es un marécage' (p.85). Such primeval fear breeds violence. It links up with Estelle's fearful statement earlier that she might drown in the bottomless pit of Inès's eyes. Such obsessions refer to the category of 'le visqueux', analysed at length in *L'Etre et le Néant*. 'C'est une activité molle, baveuse, et féminine d'aspiration, il vit obscurément sous mes doigts et je sens comme un vertige, il m'attire en lui comme le fond d'un précipice pourrait m'attirer'. Though Sartre is here talking, neurotically, of a property of matter, he clearly leaves fluid the borderline between it and female reality. He goes on: 'Le visqueux apparaît comme un liquide vu dans un cauchemar et dont les propriétés s'animeraient d'une sorte de vie et se retourneraient contre moi' (*1*, pp.700-01). In terms of imagery, male (macho) is hard, female is squidgy. The viscous, to such a mind, is especially horrific, as it is neither solid or truly liquid. It is gooey, like what Sartre comically calls in some panic 'that ignoble marmalade'.

Garcin cannot stomach the mental torture meted out to him by Inès, and he claims he would prefer the traditional physical torments of Hell. Yet, despite wanting to exit because of Inès's interrogation, he in fact opts to stay because of her. It is her, not the pliant Estelle, that he needs to convince of his non-cowardice. I say 'convince', because it is a rhetorical rather than an ethical struggle. As Champigny says, Garcin 'can only play-act as his own defender, enlisting Inès to play-act as proper judge. This can continue indefinitely [...] If Inès agrees, this will not prove that Garcin was not a coward. It will simply prove that he was a clever defender' (*8*, p.54). The living men are judging him; he therefore turns to a terminated woman to exculpate him. He persists in thinking that he can be let off the hook. All in all, he is less adaptable, that is: more stupid, in his desires than the two women.

Estelle

Liars, in daily life or on the stage, are often barefaced, and so the relative blatancy of Garcin's or Estelle's deceitfulness, compared to the more contorted version of Inès, is not inevitably a dramatic failing. When Garcin confesses how he actually behaved in a crunch-situation, Estelle does not want to hear details. She will say anything, as Inès spots, in order to keep matters only skin-deep. Estelle is always on stage, like an actress; appearances matter most to her. Early on she announces that she could not possibly sit on a spinach-green sofa when dressed in light blue. It reminds her of the vulgar décor of an old aunt (p.28). She is snobbish about the 'lower orders' (p.39). Though all three hanker for mirrors, Estelle is the most desperately avid. To feel alive at all, she depends on being registered, confirmed, by another's gaze. A mirror provides at least the semblance of making you both subject and object simultaneously, and thus puts you in some sort of control. Without a mirror, we exist nakedly under the stare of other people, which judges us and reduces us to an object.

Even before the projection-scene of current events on earth, which she cannot direct but only do a commentary on, Estelle calls up her own funeral. She has always to see and be seen: 'Quand je ne me vois pas, j'ai beau me tâter, je me demande si j'existe pour de vrai' (p.44). It is of course the admiring, not the judgmental, gaze of others that she desires. She would never second Garcin's plea for self-contained, silent introspection. Her dependence on others does not, however, imply inferiority. This narcissist had six large mirrors in her bedroom: 'Comme c'est vide, une glace où je ne suis pas. Quand je parlais, je m'arrangeais pour qu'il y en ait une où je puisse me regarder. Je parlais, je me voyais parler. Je me voyais comme les gens me voyaient, ça me tenait éveillée' (p.45). Given such self-entranced preferences, it is unsurprising that her visualizations are vindictive. Her friend Olga does not weep for Estelle's passing, as it would spoil her mascara – though Estelle admits she would behave the same herself. In the absence of a mirror, Inès offers to act as Estelle's looking-glass. Estelle sees a miniaturized version of herself in Inès's eyes (p.46).

Estelle squirms under Inès's attentions. An essential element in her bad faith is her constant reference and deference to men. When indeed Inès helps her to adjust her make-up, Estelle checks that Garcin has not noticed her misapplication (p.46). Though there appears to be a momentary sisterhood in the troubled intimacy of this scene, Estelle is unused to treating women as anything other than rivals. Inès, besides, will not resist the temptation to tease and torment Estelle by inventing a red mark on would-be flawless skin (p.48). She reminds Estelle that mirrors can tell lies.

Because surfaces matter so much to her, Estelle superficializes words. Fearing crudity, she favours euphemisms, window-dressing, verbal gentility. Euphemism presents a cosmeticized version of reality, and Estelle would die without make-up. Euphemism and bad faith, doubletalk and doublethink, feed off each other. Estelle asks Garcin to replace 'dead' with 'absent'. Ironically, a French saying has it that 'les absents ont toujours tort'. In this play, the earthly survivors put the departed trio, who cannot answer back, in the wrong. In Hell, Inès and Garcin home in on the backpedalling Estelle, forcing her into a corner. Like Garcin later, she tries to break out of the door (p.59). There is added torture, for Inès and

Garcin play pretend guessing-games about Estelle's real activities on earth; they find her predictable (p.60). In her own eyes, and though such behaviour easily becomes mechanical, Estelle claims to do always the opposite of what is expected of her. Like a petulant child, she stamps her foot, yet, like a wilful child, she holds out longest against a full admission of her guilt. She is economical with the truth.

Even when she does finally confess (she committed infanticide and thereby drove her lover to suicide), she sidesteps brass tacks. 'Il a vu des ronds sur le lac': those ripples were a sinking baby (p.61). She tries to appear offhand, as if nothing untoward had occurred. Her lover's suicide, she claims, was absurd, since her husband suspected nothing. Earlier, she had used novelettish language: 'J'ai rencontré celui que je devais aimer. Nous nous sommes reconnus tout de suite' (p.39). This pretence of fatalism tries to pass off as natural and unreprehensible both her marriage of convenience to an older man and her adulterous liaison with a young man. She has the gall to maintain that her only 'crime' was 'to sacrifice herself' to an old man, and even this is presented as a noble act to safeguard the well-being of her younger brother (p.39).

After admitting what she did on earth, Estelle becomes slightly less snobbish and permits Garcin to remain jacketless (p.62). She is still, however, bitter towards Inès for having helped to humiliate her before a man. When she resees the earth on the screen, her supposed best friend Olga is dancing with another of Estelle's admirers, Pierre. Obsessed with property, owning or being owned, Estelle is possessive about men, as Inès is about her room. Estelle remarks slightingly on Olga's ponderous breasts (p.69). She cannot but acknowledge that she has been wiped from human memory, annihilated, for her living through others makes her want also to live on in their memory.

After desertion by Pierre, she begs Garcin to catch her on the rebound (p.71). When he roughly repulses her towards Inès, she exclaims that Inès, as a mere woman, does not count. Mockingly, she spits in her face. Inter-female cattiness figures as strongly in this play as male flabbiness. At the very end, which is no end, behaving 'magically', she tries to kill the defunct Inès with the paper-knife, as though she has learned nothing of their actual situation. She has always lived selfishly through others, and will have to learn the bitterness of solitude in company.

Inès

The date of the play ensured that Inès, as a lesbian, would be portrayed in a midway position between the orthodox gender divisions. Her hostility to men counterbalances Estelle's over-reliance on them. Thus Sartre partly justifies lesbianism, if not Inès's sadomasochistic version of it. Pain, delivering it or receiving it, was her reason for existing, and, for all her boasting, such a choice can be seen only as a misuse of freedom, in that she sought to hurt and enslave others. Compared, however, with the pederast Daniel in Sartre's novel trilogy, *Les Chemins de la liberté*, who also erects himself into a satanic presence as a way of coping with his anguish, Inès seems to feel little shame. She is shameless and largely shamless. Her sidelines situation helps her to be more clear-eyed. She is the first of the three to feel definitively cut off from her previous existence, the first to see what is happening back on earth, the readiest to confess the truth, the most uncompromisingly lucid concerning everyone's guilt: 'Damnée, la petite sainte. Damné, le héros sans reproche. Nous avons eu notre heure de plaisir, n'est-ce pas? Il y a des gens qui ont souffert pour nous jusqu'à la mort et cela nous amusait beaucoup. A présent, il faut payer' (p.41). For all the pleasure she takes in harming others, on earth as in hell, she is fully aware of the link between sadism and fear. Torturers, she says (and here she anticipates Frantz von Gerlach) 'ont l'air d'avoir peur [...] Je me suis regardée dans la glace' (p.24). Garcin's nervous tics exasperate her; they are the first stage in her detection of his cowardice.

Despite her greater frankness, Inès, like the other two, is in her own way an essentialist: 'Je suis pourrie' (p.64); 'Je suis méchante' (p.57). This is the nearest she gets to taking refuge in alibis. Her evil, she claims, is a given; she was born that way, and she cannot act or be otherwise. She takes on board the conventional label of 'femme damnée', although like Sartre's version of Jean Genet, who made his own the thiefhood he was accused of, she invests her fate with passion, albeit destructive. She felt condemned while still alive, and so is better prepared than the other two for infernal punishment (p.65). For all her febrile dynamism, however, she has a passive side, as when she comments on her life on earth: 'Elle s'est mise en ordre d'elle-même' (p.33). The reflexive verb is revelatory. In fact, the only freedom she will imagine is that of choosing her own hell (p.51). Contrasting herself with Estelle's reliance on mirrors and the laudatory glances of others, Inès says: 'Je me sens toujours de l'intérieur' (p.44). This sounds more authentic, but of course she in turn depends emotionally on Estelle. For her, all relationships are painful: 'Puisqu'il faut souffrir, autant que ce soit par toi [Estelle]' (pp.45-46).

As she revels in suffering, she rejects comforting thoughts. Hell's administrators, she tells Garcin and Estelle, leave nothing to chance. Hell is 'une machine infernale', a perfect system of punishment. She piles on the agony with a blackly comic twist. Hell is a kind of lovers' tryst: 'Ils ont tout réglé. Jusque dans les moindres détails, avec amour. Cette chambre nous attendait' (p.36). Her belief in the justness of their suffering contrasts with Estelle's pathetic hanging on to the idea that they were assigned randomly together, and that she personally is the victim of a bureaucratic error (p.38). Inès adds further to their torments by singing a song, 'La Rue des Blancs-Manteaux' (written by Sartre in the 1930s and set to music by Joseph Kosma). It is a French Revolution song about guillotining aristocrats (p.43). No public executioner is of course necessary when each is 'le bourreau' of the others. The song has a circular pattern, like *Huis clos* itself. Inès's own especial torment is that the room where she and her lover Florence committed suicide (Inès involuntarily) is now being polluted by a heterosexual couple (p.64).

Inès wants in Hell to restage her terrestrial practices, to make Estelle, like her predecessor Florence, see a man (here Garcin, there Florence's husband) with Inès's hateful eyes. Her desire for Estelle

Huis clos

is her one weakness, but she needs this vulnerability in order to retain dramatic interest and plausibility. She remains the most dangerous of the three, the awkward member of the squad who upsets the applecart. Within her overall corrosive strategy she uses the tactic of offering truces. For example, if Garcin allows her free access to Estelle, she will stop needling him (p.67). On essentials, however, she is unrelenting. When Garcin persistently argues that he has done no serious wrong in his life, she forces the truth home on him. 'Seuls les actes décident de ce qu'on a voulu' (p.90). In the old saying, the road to hell is paved with good intentions. Might-have-beens are inadmissible. When he responds that he died too soon to realize his project, she coldly counters with: 'On meurt toujours trop tôt – ou trop tard. Et cependant la vie est là, terminée: le trait est tiré, il faut faire la somme. Tu n'es rien d'autre que ta vie' (p.90).[2] Vulnerable as she herself is, she passes ultimate judgment on him: 'Je ne suis rien que le regard qui te voit, que cette pensée incolore qui te pense' (p.91). Sadism here acts in the service of truth. A mere woman and her pale thoughts control a bully-boy.

'Le regard' is a major category in Sartre's Existentialist psychology. It clearly has links with the Old Testament notion of the inescapable eye of God; with the common idea of the eye of conscience (by which we keep tabs on ourselves); with the political concept of Big Brother surveilling us; or with the everyday experience of entering a room and becoming the uncomfortable focus of others' attention. Sartre's psychology is a combat of eyes/egos, or, as Iris Murdoch put it, 'a battle between hypnotists in a closed room' (*21*, p.65). Sartre harks back to the classical myth of the Gorgon/Medusa, a fabulous creature that turned to stone all she gazed upon, in order to embody his belief that *le regard* is an agent of judgment, turning a fellow subject into an object. This idea is central to *Huis clos*, where the three protagonists cannot help looking at each other: they all lack eyelids. Garcin fondly recalls the restfulness of blinking, a brief sleep: 'Un petit éclair noir, un rideau qui tombe et qui se relève: la coupure est faite. L'œil s'humecte, le

---

[2] Such final accountancy foreshadows Sartre's 1948 essay, *L'Existentialisme est un humanisme*.

monde s'anéantit. Vous ne pouvez pas savoir combien c'était rafraîchissant. Quatre mille repos dans une heure' (pp.17-18).[3] Comedy breaks into the process when Estelle attempts to use her disparaging gaze on the earthbound Olga, who is naturally immune to the would-be lethal glance of a corpse (p.70).

Amongst the dead trio, however, the gaze remains potent. Ruled by resentment, Inès's vengeful stare of course turns also inwards, against herself. Her triumphs are arid. Even in her lifetime, ironically, her slave Florence one night turned the tables on her and asphyxiated them both; Florence reasserted her freedom. Although Inès undoubtedly corrupted her own freedom by using it to imprison and brainwash her lover, such wilful behaviour clearly fascinates Sartre. He gives Inès the best lines (the devil has the catchiest tunes), the most acidic lyricism. She is a disturbing, diabolical presence.

Stage Business

Despite his many acute analyses of paintings and sculptures, Sartre remained, as the title of his autobiography, *Les Mots*, indicates, a words man. Yet the idea of Hell had to be made concrete in the play by objects. Its opening sections turn normally useful objects into intimidating, unreliable or unmovable inutilities or obstacles. They are made strange. A paper-knife, but no books to cut the pages of; a bronze statuette too massive to displace; nineteenth-century furniture in a twentieth-century Hell (Second Empire sofas, a rough equivalent of Victorian seating. Both were ages of middle-class complacency and the façade of respectable solidity); a bell that works only spasmodically; a light that cannot be switched off, representing the glare of truth; or a door that opens of itself once, but offers only apparently a moment of choice and escape, for there is truly nowhere else to go: other rooms would be merely additional mental-torture chambers. All of these things act as reminders of

---

[3] 'La coupure' refers also to electricity failure. In the Paris of rationing, the Garçon's line 'Nous avons l'électricité à discrétion' (an endless supply) convulsed the audience.

how people can be obliged to see objects no longer as convenient tools, but as dense, alien essences.[4] As Lorris stresses, the very banality of the setting of *Huis clos* underscores the horror of the situation (*17*, p.74). Normality is never experienced more poignantly than when we are deprived of it. As well as being forward-turned, Sartre's philosophy and psychology are outward-turned. He often evinces a revulsion for 'inner life', the domain of traditional psychology, because of its possible cosiness. Objects, then, like other people, are of vital significance. They are never just a backdrop, props, but an integral part of the total equation. For Sartre, our consciousness is an empty receptacle, open to fillers. Objects (think of a mountain) are challenges to measure ourselves against.

Take the bronze statuette. When Inès finally convinces Garcin that she will never let up her inquisition, he approaches the bronze. It helps to drive home to him that he is inescapably in Hell. It represents an objectification, a solid proof, of his position: he too has become a fixed essence, a coward for all time. Sartre's opposition of 'pour-soi' (consciousness) with its flimsiness and 'en-soi' (essence) with its solidity ensures that such objects exert fascination. They are what human beings can never be, though many of us long to have that secure unmovability, that exact coincidence with ourselves. Each individual risks, however, becoming thing-like, metaphorically but painfully, under the judging gaze of other individuals. The bronze is by Barbedienne, a Second-Empire bronze-caster, who specialized in production-line reduced models of well-known sculptures. As Goldthorpe comments, the statuette 'may be taken as a symbol of bourgeois philistinism and of infinite and potentially nightmarish repetition' (*14*, p.93).

As well as props, other supporting phenomena also pull their dramatic weight and add to the torment of people grating on each other's nerves. The role of the Garçon underlines the awful repetitiveness of the situation: the same old questions from an endless series of 'guests'. In the scenes relayed from earth, the three become spectators – a play within a play – and are as helpless as

---

[4] cf. *La Nausée, passim*.

playgoers to alter the dramatic action they watch. (Similar flashbacks, reenactments and dreams feature even more crucially in *Les Séquestrés d'Altona*.) What they see brings home to them the survivors' forgetfulness or indictment of the ex-mortals. They are thus punished on earth as they are in Hell. By the comments of those back on earth Sartre reverses the pious old saying: 'Never speak ill of the dead', or Horace's 'We mercifully preserve their bones and piss not upon their ashes' (*Art of Poetry*, 1.471). He matches the matter-of-fact Jules Vallès: 'La mort n'est pas une excuse'.[5]

In a variation on such scenes, the protagonists also project inner films, imagined scenarios, generally corny in character, as when Garcin concocts his wretched widow turning up loyally and forlornly at the barracks where he was executed. In its stereotyping this is self-parodying. In its unmasking of such mystifications, Sartre's theatre is iconoclastic. He tests claims against performances. 'Hypocrite' means stage-actor; *mauvaise foi* clearly relies heavily on *comédie*, and what it reveals.

Comedy and Language

Huis clos is black comedy, gallows humour. Inès is particularly adept at this excruciation. 'Eh bien, ils ont réalisé une économie de personnel. Voilà tout. Ce sont les clients qui font le service eux-mêmes, comme dans les restaurants coopératifs' (p.42). It is a self-service Hell. Each of the three laughs at some point, mockingly, drily, to accentuate the reciprocal torture. When Garcin pleads with Estelle to get him off the hook of cowardice ('nous sortirons de l'enfer', p.83), Inès bursts out laughing. The attempted murder with the paper-knife is inherently comic. What else can they all do at the end of the play, which restarts everything, but laugh, bitterly, on the other side of their faces? The situation in which they have landed themselves is more derisory than tragic. They have largely refused that lucidity which ennobles tragic sufferers, for they have tried to

---

[5] J. Vallès, quoted in F. Brunetière, *Histoire et littérature* (Gambier, n.d.), pp.291-92.

take shelter in wilful self-blindness. Their situation is absurd, and 'the absurd' can never altogether evade the sense of 'comic'. They are no longer up to being dead serious about anything. They are the dead unserious, hence their strained hilarity. In the last lines, however, the laughter falls away, as they register the ineluctable tedium of their fate.

If they can no longer change, they can still talk. The style of their acceptance or rejection of the truth – Inès the most figurative, Garcin the most abstract, Estelle the most materialistic yet also euphemistic – is still on offer for them. They talk, to persuade the others, defend themselves, or keep their morale up. McCall speaks of their 'unlivable solidarity' (*20*, p.114). They are indeed 'seuls ensemble': the perfectly cruel dramatic oxymoron (p.41). *Huis clos* is not only intensely theatrical, but also highly rhetorical: each attempts to seduce, cajole, browbeat or terrorize the others. As no true acts are possible for the dead, the whole drama relies on words. Here, words are acts. The characters carve each other up with language more effectively than Estelle can pierce Inès with the paper-knife.

Stage language, in Sartre's view, should be 'ou serment ou engagement ou refus ou jugement moral ou défense des droits ou contestation des droits des autres, donc éloquence, ou moyen de réaliser l'entreprise, c'est-à-dire menace, mensonge, etc., mais en aucun cas il ne doit sortir de ce rôle magique, primitif et sacré' (*5*, p.34). It is thus both sophisticated, like courtroom rhetoric, and yet driven by the caveman urge of self-assertion. Sartre often stressed the need for rapid, elliptical language: tit-for-tat, cut-and-thrust.

The language of Inès is the most imaged. It tears at her own wounds, as animals do, to hurt the pain. When she mocks Garcin's professed desire for mutism, she both attacks him and increases her own suffering. 'Je vous sens jusque dans mes os. Votre silence me crie dans les oreilles. Vous pouvez vous clouer la bouche, vous pouvez vous couper la langue [...] Arrêterez-vous votre pensée? Je l'entends, elle fait tic tac, comme un réveil [...] Les sons m'arrivent souillés' (p.51). Her repeated images of fire reinstate the traditional idea of Hell which Sartre otherwise modifies. Her speech is melodramatic, but passionate: 'J'ai besoin de la souffrance des autres pour exister. Une torche [...] Quand je suis toute seule, je m'éteins. Six mois durant, j'ai flambé dans son cœur [Florence]; j'ai tout brûlé' (p.57). She picks up and varies the image later on: 'Je suis sèche [...] Une branche morte, le feu va s'y mettre' (p.65). (In contrast, Estelle is liquid: '[Pierre] m'appelait son eau vive', p.68.) Fire and water obviously will not happily mix. Both sets of images no doubt typify the clichés of lovers' language, but those of Inès possess the greater destructive glee. In *Huis clos*, words cover up, and denude. The image of the three 'as naked as worms' is deadly accurate, given the graveyard implications.

Conclusion

Last words such as those of *Huis clos* – 'Eh bien, continuons' – ensure that this play does not actually end. Sartre very obviously wants it to reverberate on in the spectators' or readers' minds. But how can the three 'continue'? (There is, incidentally, an in-joke. The actors will have to repeat the same script over and over again throughout the play's run.) We could conclude that the characters have exhausted what they have to say to each other; and we could envision an ongoing, everlasting silence: a cold war, in Hell. This is Hell, nor are they out of it. Unlike many plays (though Strindberg's *Dance of Death* and Pirandello's *Henry IV* also end with the emphasis on marking time), this one hopes to elicit the response 'Doesn't it drag?' Despite lasting only about one hour twenty minutes, time here must be felt as slouching its aching feet along. Sartre does not offer us the convenient luxury or consolation of deciding that something has been resolved. Implicitly, he takes the play's receivers on as co-workers. We have our part to play. Even if *Huis clos* is unarguably pessimistic, it does strive, in a back-to-front manoeuvre, to convince us that lucidity is the first step to authentic living. Though Sartre would certainly have jibbed at what would seem to him mere exhibitionism, the idea of the three 'nus comme des vers' (p.52) could have produced in the finale three naked actors, who have stripped each other of all social and psychological camouflage: full-frontal exposure. Onlookers, for their part, can enjoy the morose delectation of watching pinned specimens squirm. The bell, however – and this one never fails to work – tolls also for us, for, if it is objected that the trio are special cases of sinful or criminal humanity, we must confess that all of us conceal something about which we could be compelled to feel shame.

What suspense can there be in the situation of stalled characters? The three wait, in dread, for something to happen. Well before the close of the play, however, they know their fate. If there is no orthodox suspense, there is suspended animation, apt for posturing corpses: they thresh about in a closed net. Besides, their shifting alignments, their unworkable, short-lived pacts, embody the politics, the diplomacy of human relations. Though this play has few obviously political dimensions – Garcin's failure to live up to his pacifist ideals does not indicate any specific favouring of pacifism – it is already clear in this early drama that for Sartre everything is inherently political, nothing totally private.

Socially, as a state employee in the postal service, Inès is a petite bourgeoise, whereas Garcin belongs to the intelligentsia, and Estelle has married into the propertied class. Politically; Garcin was in principle a committed liberal, Inès a kind of militant for her own sexual predilection. Estelle feigns to be apolitical, yet she is the most socially conditioned of the three: she truly exists only in company. Their power-relationships are intrinsically political. In present-day society, Estelle would be a Tory, pretending that politics is an activity practised only by opponents. Garcin would agonize between various choices and plump for none. Inès would lob a Molotov cocktail into the polling-station.

All acts or failures to act have repercussions on other people. We can think of the dramatic scene here as a carrousel, a dance of death, or a pinball-machine, in which people cannon off each other in continuous collisions. *Huis clos* is about the theatre of life, the acts we put on for each other. Garcin, Estelle and Inès play pointed charades.

Earlier, I called *Huis clos* a black comedy. Yet tardy awareness teamed with impotence to act decisively would seem to connect this play to the tradition of classical tragedy. Despite himself, Sartre's theatrical *nous* ensures that here even petty, rakish or smart bourgeois can be seen to suffer in exemplary fashion. To that extent, Sartre overcomes his chosen inverted snobbery which initially put all three personages beyond the pale.

3. Bridge Passage

In 1959, at the time *Les Séquestrés d'Altona* was first performed, Sartre in an interview took over Inès's harsh lesson to Garcin, and applied it to himself: 'Au théâtre, les intentions ne comptent pas. Ce qui compte, c'est ce qui *sort*' (his emphasis; *5*, p.95). What 'emerges' in this play shows several continuities, but also discontinuities, with *Huis clos*. Sartre himself said that *Les Séquestrés d'Altona* was '*No Exit* with five characters' (*6*, p.88). Inaccurately, he stressed in another interview the far heavier role of the past in the later play. In fact, the drama of *Huis clos* had depended largely on its characters' past misdeeds in order to ground their present shufflings (*4*, pp.325-26).

Both plays clearly centre on death. In the second, the Father is dying of cancer and intending suicide; Frantz is supposed to have died in Argentina and has no way out from his excruciating trap except suicide. Werner's marriage is likened to a funeral and his wife Johanna to a cadaver. In both plays, lights burn remorselessly in hell-hole prison rooms. *Les Mains sales* and the stories 'Le Mur' and 'La Chambre' also feature *huis clos* situations. In 'La Chambre' closed space offers protection for the mad. All this is intensely theatrical, because the audience is likewise locked up for the duration, and will have to re-emerge painfully into the world outside, ballasted (Sartre would hope) with shared guilt, rather than lightened by traditional catharsis.

When Leni threatens to blow the gaff on her family's shameful secrets, Frantz tries to expel her, in an unavailing reprise of the situation in *Huis clos*. Sartre, however, built new wings to Hell in the intervening years. In the later play, Hell is the world into which we are born, where we live in continuous conflict with each other. Most importantly, and with greater psychological likelihood, our choices are seen as no longer entirely ours. Yet guilt and responsibility still dominate both plays. In terms of relationships, in each play characters pursue each other despairingly and never properly coincide in a balance. In sexual matters, incest takes over from lesbianism as a heroic variation from the norm. Lastly, both plays give a large part to lies, which introduce suspicion, suspense and conflict. Hell in both plays would be dramatically more static without the tensions brought in by passionate lying, to oneself as much as to others.

Sartre's first attempt at drama, *Bariona*, written when he was a prisoner-of-war, logically centred (like the two later plays under discussion) on captives, under surveillance, in a fenced space. As in *Les Séquestrés d'Altona*, Sartre was already combining a form of allegory with distancing effects, in both cases so as to sidestep censorship. His first dramatic experience taught him the lasting lesson of the theatre as a locus of group-work (author, actors, director, backstage staff and audience), as a way to gaining an immediate, visible, palpable effect on its receivers. When Sartre saw his fellow prisoners 'soudain si remarquablement silencieux, je compris ce que le théâtre devrait être: un grand phénomène collectif et religieux' (*5*, p.62). In a 1951 interview, Sartre said that it was behind barbed wire that he properly understood what real freedom is.[6] Above all, Sartre always valued the theatre as the very embodiment of human ambiguity: flesh-and-blood actors in fictional situations against artificial backdrops which aim to give a stylized illusion of reality.

---

[6] Sartre, interview with G. d'Aubarède, *Les Nouvelles littéraires*, 1 Feb. 1951.

4. Les Séquestrés d'Altona

The play's title is loaded. Within the play, reference is made to one of Werner's cases involving sequestration. After Frantz has called her 'une séquestrée', for this outsider appears trapped in the family house, ethos and hopelessness, Johanna picks up that reference: 'J'ai vu la fille d'un client de Werner: enchaînée, trente-cinq kilos, couverte de poux. Je lui ressemble?' To which Frantz responds: 'Comme une sœur. Elle voulait tout, je suppose' (p.193). The last phrase, a curious conclusion to jump to, indicates that Sartre lifted the idea from Gide's *La Séquestrée de Poitiers*, for Gide suggests that the sequestered girl he studied willed her imprisonment. In 1901, a girl was discovered in filth and semi-idiocy, locked up in a respectable bourgeois apartment. Evident parallels between Gide's reportage and Sartre's play include: the mottoes on the walls of the room, the morbid fear of objects, a schizophrenic mixture of childishness and sophistication, of purity and obscenity. In Poitiers, investigators found that the whole well-to-do family had unhealthy affinities with filth. In the 1930s, Sartre followed up his deep interest in madness by visits to an asylum, extensive readings in psychoanalytical literature, and experiments with the hallucinogenic drug, mescalin. In 1957, in his review *Les Temps Modernes*, Sartre published a long essay on the painter Tintoretto, called 'Le Séquestré de Venise', in which the subject is described in these terms: 'Accusé volontaire, le malheureux s'est engagé dans un procès sans fin; il assurera lui-même sa défense, il fait de chaque tableau un témoin à décharge. Il plaide, il ne cesse de plaider'.[7] Sartre's Tintoretto is self-sequestered, like Frantz von Gerlach.

Sartre wanted to give this recurrent obsession a strong historical, even topical, dimension. While it might seem

---

[7] Sartre, 'Le Séquestré de Venise', *Les Temps Modernes*, 141 (1957), 792.

contradictory to write for your time, with all the risks of dating involved, and simultaneously attempt a mythic distancing, this was in fact Sartre's decision. Early in 1958, Sartre was clearly edging towards what would become the plot of the play: 'A play on the decomposition that can result in a family from the silence maintained by a conscript on his return from Algeria' (*4*, pp.319-20). When the play was put on, however, he denied the link, both because the Algerian War was still in an acute phase and he feared censorship, and because of his wish to widen his topic. Hence his switch of setting from France to Germany. He still argued that the play dealt with a general dilemma: the stricken conscience of a soldier led by circumstances to go too far in his military duties (*4*, pp.328-29). In yet another interview, he extended his play's scope with the provocative declaration that nobody in a society that has become repressive is exempt from the risk of involvement with torture (*4*, pp.330-31). What is at stake here is the question of collusion, which can clearly embrace civilians with soldiers or police.

When writing this play, Sartre was exhausted by his labours on his major political work, *Critique de la raison dialectique*. He was taking benzedrine copiously, dropping objects all over the place. He was in a truly piteous state, and in fact had to stop all work for several months. He reworked *Les Séquestrés d'Altona* several times. It cost his mind and body much more to write than any other of his plays.

The Play and History

Sartre's *Critique de la raison dialectique* is an elaborate attempt to fuse elements of Existentialism, Marxism and the psychoanalytical theories of Freud. In comparison with *L'Etre et le Néant* of two decades earlier, it complicates and makes more realistic his analysis of human freedom, by introducing numerous factors which severely limit the earlier, more idealistic, though extremely challenging version of freedom. These factors include principally the whole economic basis of life, which in turn determines political reality, which for its part crucially influences individuals, to a large extent via their families, who are the active intermediaries between the self, society and the wider world. No longer, then, is it a matter of self-assertion in a social vacuum, or of willing one's independence from others, but rather of struggling on the same unsure footing as them in local, national and indeed global conflicts.

The guiding argument in *Critique de la raison dialectique* owes a great deal to Marx. Within the capitalist system, man's efforts to dominate matter, whether raw materials in a factory or nature in agriculture, readily turn against him. He signs away his labour into what he produces. In *Les Séquestrés d'Altona*, the von Gerlach industrial empire typifies this process, at the level of the company owner rather than at that of the grass-roots worker. Secondly, the son Frantz's act of torture, which Sartre sees as the attempt to convert human beings into brute matter, also backfires and returns to haunt him, and eventually to drive him to death. What Sartre terms in the *Critique* the 'pratico-inert' is the synthesis of lifeless matter and human activity. In his use, it takes on a highly threatening character. We should recognize, however, the widespread anxiety today that machines (e.g. computers) are increasingly controlling their human operators. In recent stock-market crises, even financial experts have confessed to a sense that no-one was in charge, that a process was operating by its own impetus. Presumably, for Marx or for Sartre, in a post-capitalist world human work would not backlash in this way, would not engender dehumanization.

If the non-human menaces, humankind does so even more. Capitalism depends on scarcity to create value, and rarity leads to exploitation, competition and violence. Man is 'l'espèce carnassière' (*2*, p.208). In the play, the starving prison-camp inmates, or the orphan from bombed Düsseldorf who plagues Frantz's delirium, embody this fact of life. People also behave self-destructively, like the Chinese peasants who, desperate for firewood, stripped forests, which led to desertification. Sartre calls this economic irony 'contre-finalité'; more colloquially, it is Sod's Law. Present-day ecologists brandish much damning evidence at the mass of mankind who produce results that no-one anticipated or desired. In family terms, counter-finality can take the form of begetting children, in the hope that they may take after us, and then having to watch them grow away, into independence. Dialectical reasoning (i.e. two-way, reciprocal) ensures that Frantz counter-accuses his father of building into his training of his son his own crimes against humanity. For his part, the Father knows (he is an inadequate God: wellnigh omniscient, but as near as dammit powerless) that in life nothing stands still, despite his own essentialist urges – his efforts to secure stasis via continuity of succession in the firm, his desire to make son repeat father. The Enterprise, he knows, will not remain in the family's hands forever, and is very likely to be nationalized (p.58). It is, moreover, intrinsically back-to-front, a living paradox, crazy (though there is method in its madness). As the Father explains to his other son, Werner, referring to Gelber, the perfect company-man: 'C'est ton employé: tu le paies pour qu'il te fasse connaître les ordres que tu dois donner' (p.31). Not only Frantz but also capitalism itself is schizophrenic. Sartre annexes the Marxist argument that capitalism is riddled with internal contradictions.

Les Séquestrés d'Altona, though distanced geographically from France, is topical in terms of historical reference. Sartre's version of history pictures it as inherently ambiguous. Indeed, one of the major themes of the play is how history, the unrolling of events in time, perpetually takes us aback, shatters our expectations or wishes. The four countries the play alludes to, Germany, France, Algeria and Soviet Russia, were all, for different reasons, of major importance to Sartre: his heavy debt to German philosophy, his French nationality, his anticolonialism, and his political stance as a critical fellow-traveller to Communism. We could easily add other possible dimensions: the USA in Vietnam, Britain in Northern Ireland. As well as attacking capitalism, the play also attacks Communism, which has recently gone into apparently terminal decline. Sartre told Tynan in 1961 that his play was tied up with the whole evolution of Europe since 1945, as much with Soviet concentration-camps as with the war in Algeria (*4*, pp.366-67). Krushchev's speech in 1956 accused Stalin of crimes which, like

Frantz's on the Eastern Front, or France's in Algeria, turned out to be not only evil, but also unnecessary, unproductive. As Thody points out, 'Frantz's action in torturing the [Russian] partisans is like Hugo's shooting of Hoederer [in *Les Mains sales*]. Because of a twist in the direction history has taken, it becomes a crime which nobody wants' (*29*, p.119). That is, a politically useless and embarrassing act. *Les Séquestrés d'Altona* pays much homage to the so-called verdict of history (i.e. of posterity). But we may well wonder why 'history' should be any more definitively correct in its judgments in the future here-and-now than people were in the past.

For Verstraeten, in Sartre's eyes 'l'histoire passe toujours par l'individu: on a la guerre qu'on mérite, et les névroses de son époque' (*31*, p.197). This analysis places the ball firmly back in the individual's court. On the evidence of this play, we fumble in the dark about the possible validity of our decisions and actions. There are no pre-established values in the past or present, and no means of taming the future. We seem to be left largely with attitudes to the past (as in *Huis clos*), styles of responsibility or abdication. *Les Séquestrés d'Altona* offers little hope of effective acts, of change. The biggest enemy of Sartre's characters (and *Les Mots* harps unrelentingly on this theme) is unreality: gestures instead of true acts, putting on performances for others, solo performances. In the play, the options are heavily loaded. As Johanna says to her husband Werner, on the question of protecting or denouncing Frantz, which would land them too in court: 'A nous de choisir: nous serons les domestiques du fou qu'ils te préfèrent ou nous nous assoirons sur le banc des accusés. Quel est ton choix? Le mien est fait: la cour d'assises. Mieux vaut la prison à terme que le bagne à perpétuité' (p.51). In fact, she will not see this so-called choice through. Our acts escape our clutches. Johanna says to Frantz: 'Donc chacun fait le contraire de ce qu'il veut?' To which he responds: 'Que chacun veuille ce qu'il est contraint de faire' (p.278). His response suggests that we can at best play ball with our fate. The only freedom left is that of assuming what has determined you: you must answer and pay for your past acts. Most of the time, this play's protagonists are less 'en train de se faire' than 'en train de se défaire'. Ten years earlier, in *Qu'est-ce que la litterature?*, Sartre was already stating: 'Les héros sont des libertés prises au piège, comme nous tous' (*3* (*2*), p.313). Freedom, for Sartre, is always a beyond, imaginable if not yet feasible. As in 'Le Mur', a brick wall thwarts our activity, which is maybe what Sartre meant when he said: 'Il faut porter sur la scène des situations-limites' (*5*, p.20).

In order to counteract such deep pessimism, Sartre converts to the atheistic, humanistic cause the wager proposed by the Christian apologist Pascal. (Why not bet on God's existence? What have you to lose?) Gambling is an insistent leitmotif in *Les Séquestrés d'Altona*, for which an alternative title was *Qui perd gagne*. Loser takes all. The defeated Germany (or Japan) underwent an economic miracle. By implication, France should take a chance on granting Algeria independence. Such a loss might pay off in time, in terms of good diplomatic relations, trade, etc. On the other hand, military oppression and atrocities will pay no 'peace dividend'.

The other side of the medal, of course, is winner takes nothing – the pointlessness of Frantz's torturing, or the personal fall of the mighty magnate, his father. And an awkward question: if loser takes all, what does Frantz, the born loser, take? In a more disabused and moderate variation, the Father admits: 'on ne gagne jamais; j'essaie de sauver la mise' (p.338). But he cannot 'get his money back'. The die has been cast. A further dimension of the gambling image concerns placing cards on the table: frankness. Sartre presents the family as the last place to expect honest dealings, candid exchanges. Not only Frantz but everyone else utters unreliable, several-edged statements, so that when Leni says: 'Abattez votre jeu', she knows in her bones this can never happen (p.107). Each is playing poker against the rest. Who will hold the master-cards (p.106)? Sartre is incapable of the debonair acceptance of life's dealings and sleights of hand exhibited by Diderot in a more confident Age of Enlightenment: 'Je ne saurai qu'à la fin ce que j'aurai perdu ou gagné dans ce vaste tripot, où j'aurai passé une soixantaine d'années, le cornet à la main, *tesseras agitans* [shaking the dice]'.[8]

---

[8] D. Diderot, *Eléments de physiologie*, vol. 9 of *Œuvres complètes*, edited by J. Assézat (Garnier, 1875), p. 428.

Sartre and Diderot meet, however, in that both leave us up in the air, but with our feet mired in the ground, which is likely to give way at any moment. They are profoundly unsettling writers.

The Family

Since starting work on *Les Mots* in the mid-Fifties, Sartre had placed a new and heavy emphasis on the family – in this play, the dynasty. This new direction stemmed from autobiographical reasons, but equally from his increasing sense of the family as the crucial go-between linking individual and society. With his lifelong passionate interest in Greek tragedy, the insistent theme of family pride concealing family crimes informs his attempt to lift the von Gerlachs to tragic status. Their *hubris* (overweening pride) is their *hamartia* (tragic flaw). In this way, the domestic can rise to the level of the mythological. We might also recall two linked samples of folk wisdom: 'Keep it in the family' (whether wealth or secrets), and 'Do not wash your dirty linen in public'. Despite or because of Frantz's ethical exhibitionism, his self-lacerating tape-recordings which could become public knowledge after his death, he eventually helps to destroy his family from the inside, in Japanese fashion, by ritual joint suicide with his father.

Ritual, and vestigial religion, play important parts. Thody analyses at some length the numerous Christian references – from the oath on the family Bible, to the theme of the father creating the son in his own image, and the son himself as a Prodigal Son, or, again, as a Samson; the role of the Protestant leader, Luther; the atmosphere of Judgment Day (*28*, pp.216-18). For my part, I believe that Sartre's atheism was firm and constant; that for him too an atheist is a person with no invisible means of support. For this reason, and on the evidence of how such religious allusions are exploited dramatically in the play, I take them to be principally parodic. Cutting up the cake Leni brings him, Frantz blasphemes against Communion: 'Ceci est mon corps' (p.316). When he eats this Host, he chokes on it, calling it 'un étouffe-coquin' (p.320) – a regional variant for 'étouffe-chrétien', i.e. stodgy food. Sartre himself, however, readily admitted to his affinities with Protestants (and a forbear was Albert Schweitzer). He always felt better understood by them, as, in his view, they shared his preoccupation with individual responsibility and likewise refused intercessors. Obviously, it is French or German Protestants he has in mind, and not the lukewarm English variety, when he praises their all-or-nothing outlook (see *5*, p.323 and *4*, p.331). In *Les Séquestrés d'Altona*, the Protestant lieutenant Klages is, however, accused by Frantz of the escapism reputedly practised by Jesuits, 'mental reservations' (p.303).

Furthermore, Sartre links Lutheranism with manic pride (p.76). Economic historians like Max Weber have many times stressed the tight bonds between the rise of capitalism and that of Protestantism. In this perspective, the capitalist feels a God-given vocation to make money, to the greater glory of God. (Though present-day capitalists would largely shun such a religious filiation, they certainly make a fetish out of wealth-creation.) The von Gerlachs no longer hold genuine religious beliefs, but they cling to pseudo-religious rituals, like the oath sworn on the family Bible. This in turn is a parody of the revolutionary oath that Sartre studies in *Critique de la raison dialectique* – sworn by a group protesting against fragmentation. The von Gerlachs can offer only a sham of such valid, binding oaths, for, behind its façade, this family group is falling to pieces. As Leni comments, 'Les principes s'en vont, les habitudes restent' (p.15), and again: 'Cette famille a perdu ses raisons de vivre, mais elle a gardé ses bonnes habitudes' (p.23). Its observances are thus an empty shell. Excruciatingly, the Father insists 'pas des cérémonies' (p.24), for the family is in fact hogtied by outdated conventions. Even more ironically, it is the Father, the God-like Father, who declares towards the close that the Almighty does not exist: 'C'est même parfois bien embêtant' (p.348). Or, as Beckett's Hamm less suavely exclaims: 'Le salaud! Il n'existe pas!'[9]

---

[9] S. Beckett, *Fin de partie* (Minuit, 1957), p.76.

The Father

In the Father, Sartre blends bourgeois paternity and capitalist paternalism. He mixes in psychoanalysis, for the cigars he consumes and the cancer relate him to the founding father, Freud. For his part, Frantz addresses Hitler as 'petit père' (p.137). In *Les Séquestrés d'Altona*, politics, history and the family are all richly and hopelessly entangled. The play opens lengthily, in edgy expectation. A son, daughter and daughter-in-law, two insiders and a semi-outsider, are waiting for God, a god no longer worthy of reverence, but still dreaded. Like Communism for so many intellectuals, the God that failed. To create him, Sartre truly flogged his imagination and empathy, for von Gerlach is a much more complex and at times moving figure than the city-fathers ('Salauds!') of *La Nausée*, or the two-dimensional father/factory boss of 'L'Enfance d'un chef'. As Contat argues, the father would be utterly odious and virtually comic, if the whole play is not seen as a tragedy centered as much on him as on his son Frantz (*9*, p.55). Pathetically, he implores Leni and Johanna to help him (p.105). In a stage direction, Sartre writes: 'A présent qu'il est seul, il ne se maîtrise plus, et visiblement, il souffre' (p.215).

A manipulator (he has, like his son, a tic of rubbing his hands together, like the Dickensian hypocrite, Uriah Heep), he adroitly manoeuvres Leni and Johanna, since dictatorship over the family is his one remaining area of real power. (As for his business-empire, 'Il y a beau temps que je ne décide plus rien', p.30.) Leni talks of the delayed-action bomb he has placed in their home (p.213), though Johanna contradicts: 'Votre machine infernale va vous éclater entre les mains' (p.230). The bitter ironies of his situation ensure that the Father's humour is black: 'Dans six mois, j'aurai tous les inconvénients d'un cadavre sans en avoir les avantages' (p.25). Cancer is the other ticking bomb. He announces that he is medically 'condamné', before we find out that he is also ethically, politically, existentially damned. Like Garcin in *Huis clos*, he longs, in his remaining six months, to put his affairs in order (p.75), that is: to arrange his succession, and to see his son for the first and last time in many years. Not only capitalism but also Nature is backfiring. He will die of 'une mort industrielle: la Nature pour la dernière fois rectifiée' (p.25). His lucidity is, however, entirely negative; it cannot lead to new, effective action, except suicide.

Though ostensibly outmanoeuvring the others, he is in effect gambling. His desperate urge to see his son could fail at any moment and, even if it succeeds, it will be a hollow triumph: winner will take nothing, except their paired lives. As well as gambling metaphors, he also exploits the language of accountancy. 'Si je le revois, j'arrête le compte et je fais l'addition [...] Il faut que je tire le trait moi-même, sinon tout s'effilochera' (p.104). Like the inveterate businessman he is, he always offers deals, contracts, and is ready to be flexible in negotiations (e.g. p.231).

This captain of industry now become an anachronism has no forename. He is the Father, embodiment of a vitiated form of paternity, and the medium through which the Enterprise rules the whole family. Despite his worship of (economic) progress, he is in fact an essentialist: 'Werner est faible, Frantz est fort: personne n'y peut rien' (p.54). Leni nicknames him 'le vieil Hindenburg', after the president of the Weimar Republic which Hitler overthrew in 1933: a man of erstwhile power reduced to a mere figurehead (p.14). Johanna converts the term for this ('homme de paille') to 'patrons de paille' (straw bosses), when she envisages Werner taking over the business (p.40). Yet the Father survives, empty but ponderous. Marx wrote powerfully on such vampirism from the past. In the preface to *Capital*: 'We suffer not only from the living but from the dead. Le mort saisit le vif!' [10]

Ironically powerless in his terminal state, the Father had in the past pursued power for its own sake: the 'natural' right, so close to a 'divine' right, to rule. This was balanced, complacently, by that sense of duty enshrined in paternalism. Sartre told Tynan that 'le désir de garder le pouvoir vient de ce qu'on le possède déjà' (5, p.156). It is no doubt callously heartening for the average citizen to

---

[10] K. Marx, preface to *Capital*, translated by B. Fowkes, vol. 1 (Harmondsworth: Penguin, 1976), p. 91.

witness how power can become a prisonhouse. Nazism was made possible by the ideology of the natural right of the strong, the 'master-race', to lord it over and ultimately to eliminate the weak. It was assented to by Werner-like citizens. Like many of his social class, the Father was not a committed Nazi and was indeed contemptuous of the uppity Hitler. But he bandwaggoned. The Nazis created markets for his products (p.77); the imperatives of capitalism pushed him to collaboration. In other words, he behaved with perfect cynicism, arguing that the end – the success of his firm – justified the means. The logic of his choice made him grant a tract of land on his estate to the Nazis for a concentration-camp (p.71). When Frantz sheltered a runaway Jew from the camp, the Father got him off the legal hook, so as to protect both him and the business, by denouncing the Jew. The Father was abdicating his selfhood, in Sartre's view. He became an Other, in a process of 'altérité'. Like 'alter' in English, *altérer* means to make other. In *Critique de la raison dialectique*, Sartre analyses 'altérité sérielle'. This is a kind of production-line on which we let ourselves embark. It is mankind seen as a mass of artificially clustered atoms, each in conflict with the rest in a regime of scarcity. The true horror of this situation is that humans can, like Frantz, feel both innocent and guilty. We do not intend what happens, and yet we recognize our responsibility for it. The Father instructs Werner: 'Si tu veux commander, prends-toi pour un autre', and he adds that a week after the Father's death, Werner will be an exact replica of him (pp.29-30). Werner's inheritance will be an alien self. Before granting land to the Nazis, the Father had the choice of saving himself, but he spurned it. He yielded to what it suited him to believe was a necessity. He freely chose complicity, and became a hostage to a system.

Leni

Leni is no less trapped than her father, though she wriggles frantically in her chains, before she ends up making a virtue of necessity by totally accepting her bondage. She is indeed the most sequestered of them all, because she refuses to acknowledge that anything fundamentally wrong resides in self-sequestration. In the von Gerlach scheme of things, women are due to play only a subordinate role (there is but one brief mention of the dead mother). They are treated largely as adjuncts or decoration. Leni herself is allowed immunity from seriousness; and Johanna is employed to suit her father-in-law's purposes, which play on the hoary stereotype of the beautiful temptress. Werner explains to Johanna, with pious hopefulness: 'Chez les Gerlach, les femmes se taisent' (p.38). While holding essentially the same view, the Father is more subtly flexible in his attitude towards and his exploitation of the two women. In dramatic terms, however, the two women are vitally central to the entire course of events in the play. They provoke change in what would otherwise be a stalemate.

Leni harbours violently mixed emotions about the family, the house, her father. She is bound by her very hatreds. While verbally rebellious, she has, of course, stayed put. As Contat comments, 'Leni est réduite à jouer la comédie de la révolte [...] Elle est enfermée dans la prison sans barreaux de l'attitude mentale de refus crispé et inefficace qu'elle a adoptée' (9, pp.38-39). Much of the time, she chooses to inhabit the imaginary realm of fantasy, where everything seems possible. This is akin to schizophrenia: the holding of the real and the fantasmal in balance or more often in alternation. She is living, in effect, a lie, and refusing to leave the room which is in many respects a madman's cell. In addition to lying to herself, she acts as an unreliable go-between for others. She perverts or invents the messages she bears. When caught out having misdescribed Johanna, she persists in her previous view: 'Oui: elle a le dos droit. Ça n'empêche pas qu'elle soit bossue' (p.319). More seriously, and here the lie seeks to brainwash, she tries to forestall Johanna's incursion into Frantz's room by making out that a murderess is on her way (p.134).

She makes a passionate defence of lying, which she sees as heroic. She says to her brother Werner: 'Je donnerais mon âme et ma peau pour l'homme que j'aimerais, mais je lui mentirais toute ma vie, s'il le fallait' (p.44). This is in effect what she does with

Frantz, sustaining, for instance, the idea that Germany in 1959 is still in ruins (p.141). This is their 'délire à deux' which parallels that of Johanna and Frantz. Like Estelle, she is ready to say anything to preserve the status quo, including the sham oath on the Bible, or informing Frantz's imaginary crab tribunal that she venerates them (p.186). More than of Estelle, Leni is, however, a reprise and an extension of Inès: feisty, butch, bolshy. Despite her febrile energy, nonetheless, she is static, an essence. Her father truly says of her: 'Tu ne changeras jamais, Leni. Quoi qu'il arrive' (p.211). All the same, and although she desperately loves Frantz, she reintroduces time into his would-be timeless space by bringing in that day's newspaper with its article on the German economic miracle (p.323).

Her variability, within that unchangingness, makes her a dangerous presence. Her playfulness skates on thin ice. When after the War she aroused Americans billeted on her family, she then whispered to them: ' "Je suis nazie", en les traitant de sales juifs', as her father recalls (p.90). When one US soldier attempted to rape this part-time *allumeuse*, Frantz intervened and Leni hospitalized the GI by cracking his head with a bottle. As with the incident of the sheltered rabbi, the Father again 'fixed' this problem facing his two children, and the subterfuge of Frantz emigrating to Argentina was concocted.

Her main function is to keep Frantz 'éveillé. Voilà vingt ans qu'il est minuit dans le siècle: ça n'est pas très commode de garder les yeux ouverts à minuit' (p.152).[11] It must be said that Leni blinds Frantz to reality, even if she keeps him awake; and she wilfully shuts her own eyes. Vaingloriously, she claims to be deliriously happy with Frantz: 'le bonheur fou' (p.106). In a 1960 interview, Sartre said that he deliberately picked an incestuous relationship. 'Il

---

[11] This is another reference back to *Huis clos* and its eyelidless characters, but also to Victor Serge's novel, *S'il est minuit dans le siècle* (1939), centred on 1934, a dark year when both Stalin and Hitler were consolidating their totalitarian regimes. The hero of Serge's novel takes upon himself the onus of a trumped-up charge against fellow-dissidents, but then escapes to continue the struggle.

fallait un élément égoïste, aveugle' (*5*, p.319). His premiss seems to be that incest is more passionate, and certainly more amoral, than orthodox love. In *Les Mots* (Gallimard, 1964, pp.41-42), Sartre describes feeling for his mother as for an elder sister, because her father treated her as a child. It was taboos that appealed to him, going against the grain, rather than any physically erotic kink. Similarly, in *Les Séquestrés d'Altona*, when Leni boasts of her incest with Frantz ('Tu n'as pas couché avec moi?'), he replies deflatingly: 'Si peu' (pp.148-49). For him, paltry in meaning as much as in frequency, no doubt. Buoyed up by her family pride ('Je suis née Gerlach, cela veut dire: folle d'orgueil'), she persists in asserting their incest: 'C'est ma loi, c'est mon destin' (p.186). She sounds like a good Existentialist when she declares: 'J'ai fait ce que j'ai voulu et je veux ce que j'ai fait' (p.150), but her wilfulness has had such little effet, except on her own morale. Williams has suggested that the incest of Leni and Frantz might reflect Nazi Germany's attempt to ignore reality by turning inward and seeking to protect itself against impure mingling, for instance with Jews (*32*, p.65). Above all, I believe that incest appeared to Sartre as risk-taking defiance.

Johanna

More bifurcating forms of incest involve Johanna. Lumping together her husband Werner and Frantz, she says: 'Chacun cherche sur moi les caresses de l'autre' (p.265). Incest in its widest sense indeed dominates this household of inward-turned people, living through each other, or via a third. It is true that Johanna tries to break the vicious circle of the family, having broken into it, but she gets embroiled. In horror at Frantz's crime, she will later back out, only to be recaught in her function/destiny as Werner's wife. She has real intelligence, but she does not convert it into effective action. After listening to the story of the rescued then betrayed Jew, she comments pointedly: '[Frantz] a compris qu'on lui permettait tout parce qu'il ne comptait pour rien' (pp.88-89). In other words, she has seen the common thread between Frantz's early impotence

Les Séquestrés d'Altona

and his later military attempt at omnipotence. Like Inès, she sees more clearly than the family insiders, the home team, the true infernal nature of the situation. She says to Frantz: 'Vous ne comprenez rien. Nous allons souffrir l'Enfer' (p.260).

Johanna shuttles, then, like Eve in 'La Chambre', between two worlds, two competing lies and prisons – upstairs and ground floor. She pleads with Werner to take her away from the accursed house, as if her own two feet did not suffice (p.246). She is undeceived, or less deceived, as when she tells the Father that she and Frantz, 'Nous nous entendons. Comme larrons en foire' (p.218). They practise, that is, reciprocal robbery, as well as straining for 'un délire à deux'. And yet, until she learns the truth about his wartime behaviour, she sees in him a contradictory mixture: 'Un traître. Inspiré. Convaincant' (p.226). For Contat, both she and Frantz are 'assoiffés d'Absolu' (*9*, p.48), though in practice their would-be all-or-nothingness is riddled with compromise and self-contradiction. In Sartre's eyes, her former profession as an actress both makes and breaks her. She was a star, and thus special; but she never coincided with her status. There is no mention of acting ability, only of beauty. 'Il sont venus me dire que j'étais belle et je les ai crus' (p.119). She sat in cinemas, sensed the audience's excitement at her appearance, but 'Je n'ai jamais vu ce qu'ils voyaient' (p.196). This beauty, besides being in the eye of the beholder, was also synthetic. 'On me faisait une ... beauté. Une par film' (p.118). Make-up artificially created her. Her consciousness, in classic Existentialist fashion, acted as a separating agent, preventing coincidence with a self. Play-acting was the 'natural' consequence of this failure to achieve full being. Actors of either gender often ruefully admit that they hardly have a face, or a self, to call their own; they exist most vitally in their roles. In their own luxurious way, they are every bit as alienated as any worker under capitalism. Johanna's obsession with beauty, which is her *folie*, though less self-assured than Estelle's, serves to link her with the earlier figure, though Johanna is clearly more complex than her forerunner. Neither she or Frantz are total dupes of the *comédie* they perform for each other.

Les Séquestrés d'Altona was, perhaps wrongly, first trailered as *L'Amour*. This title would not have come amiss. Father/Frantz, Leni and Johanna/Frantz: this play is as much about love in some of its myriad forms as about politics and history. Frantz hopes to wrest human love and especially forgiveness for his crimes from Johanna. (The inhuman crabs of his imaginary tribunal never respond.) Her horror at the full exposure of his crimes is, however, that of the 'belle âme' that Sartre always loathed – and accused Camus of being: that is, an ethical idealist who secretes fine feelings but does not take any positive action.

In *L'Etre et le Néant*, Sartre had typified love as two free subjects seeking a transcendent unity (*1*, p.433). By this he meant that each sought simultaneously to be oneself and the other person. He adds that such a goal is unreachable in theory, let alone in practice. Johanna and Frantz parody what is already an impossible ideal. When Johanna speaks of 'un délire à deux' (p.201), she picks up his earlier offer of a deal: 'C'est un marché: "Entrez dans ma folie, j'entrerai dans la vôtre"' (p.197). For his part, Frantz claims that she and he are of a kind: 'Les séquestrés disposent de lumières spéciales qui leur permettent de se reconnaître entre eux' (p.192). A little later, more enigmatically, he says: 'La mort est le miroir de la mort. Ma grandeur reflète votre beauté' (p.198). However captivating their desperate clinging to each other's love, their fencing, their mutual play-acting, their dialogue often veer into Existentialist *marivaudage*: paradoxical, patterned conceits. Their 'folie à deux' is reciprocal bad faith.

In such love, as in hell, there is no way out. 'Nous ne pouvons ni mourir ni vivre' (p.273). What is more, their duet of madness threatens his private, possibly saving, schizophrenia. Frantz warns Johanna: 'Vous me détruirez lentement, sûrement, par votre seule présence. Déjà ma folie se délabre; Johanna, c'était mon refuge' (p.276). This is another counter-finality, or unintended result. Her trying to love Frantz risks destabilizing his very shaky hold on life.

To the extent that she succeeds in loving him, Johanna proves, nevertheless, that he is worthy of love, though also that he must face up to judgment. Perhaps only an exceptional parent or sibling can survive the shock of moral horror and offer blanket pardon. Johanna finally grows lugubrious, wills herself into passivity and, so doing, seems to abdicate the sharp intelligence she had displayed earlier. She says to Werner that the mad tell the truth (p.245). This is no doubt sometimes true, but is no guide to conduct. The only 'truth' she can instance is 'l'horreur de vivre' (p.246). There has throughout been something deathly in Johanna: her beauty, which was no real part of her, was a cold cod. The fact remains that, as the Father recognizes, and he indeed engineers the process, this outsider is the catalyst that injects change into the stalled family (see p.45).

Despite all the vehement, despairing love between Father and son, between siblings, or between Frantz and Johanna, none of the protagonists, except when Johanna makes to lacerate Frantz's face, will willingly touch, or be touched by, another. The Father flinches from Werner, Leni from her father's caresses, Frantz from Leni's. When he allows her once to stroke his face, he soon leaps away, shouting: 'A distance! A distance respectueuse. Et surtout pas d'émotion' (p.147). The severely immature Hugo in *Les Mains sales* similarly dreads physical contact. Behind such touch-me-not purism lurks no doubt a mistrust of one's own body, as at least potentially an alien thing (cf. *La Nausée*). And a fear of reality, for nothing is more down-to-earth than a human body. It is symptomatic that the true madman, Pierre, in 'La Chambre', is retractile, mortally horrified of being pressed by another's flesh. No wonder that Frantz tries to minimize his bouts of incestuous intercourse with Leni.

Werner

Of all the characters, Werner suffers most from rejection. For most of the play, he is indeed, as Contat put it, the stooge, the straight man (*9*, p.42): he is on the receiving end. In dynasties such as his, a younger son is merely a fail-safe provision, a reserve. Werner loves his father, who scorns him, as Johanna points out, but her husband has always known it in his bones: 'Je vous ai répugné dans ma chair du jour où je suis né' (p.52). It is only partly true to say, as Contat does: 'Au contraire de Leni qui a choisi de se préférer en se donnant raison contre le monde entier, Werner, lui, a choisi de se donner radicalement tort: il est pénétré du sentiment de son indignité' (*9*, p.42). While being obedience personified, Werner is an essential part of the dialectical system, which needs the weak for the bullies to tyrannize. And yet ironically, amidst all the Nazi Superman talk of 'survival of the fittest', Werner, the least fit, is the one to survive. Here again, loser takes all, though much good may it do him.

He has enjoyed a successful career as a lawyer, and initially charmed Johanna into marriage. He tastes freedom when away from the forbidding mansion, but always on his return his subordinate position is brought home to him. In a variation on the family oath, he has effectively signed away his whole life to fulfil his father's wishes. Leni's cutting judgment on him is: 'Je déteste les victimes quand elles respectent leurs bourreaux' (p.16). Hearing the account of the murdered rabbi, Werner says to the Father: 'Père, je vous approuve sans réserve' (p.87). One of his vestigial real emotions is his jealous grievance against his elder brother. Even here, though, such resentment leads him to live through his brother, to try to live up to him (see p.43). It suits his parasitical nature to become (titular) head of the Enterprise. At the end, all the same, he experiences no triumph, since such a post in fact sequesters him in turn. He is, besides, drinking more and more, guzzling champagne, like Frantz. This lawyer's end-position is a life-sentence.

It is perfect bad faith for Werner to complain to his father: 'Est-ce ma faute si vous ne m'avez enseigné que l'obéissance passive?' (pp.28-29). Though he moans a great deal, in his heart he acquiesces. He takes shelter in the claim of ordinariness: 'Je suis un homme comme les autres. Ni fort ni faible, n'importe qui' (p.56). Such worms can of course turn. His deep rancour against his brother leads Werner to behave like a pathetically violent male chauvinist pig towards Johanna: 'Vous n'aimez que la force, vous autres femmes. Et la force, c'est moi qui l'ai' (p.247). This couple had been coming unstuck from early on in the play; it takes time for Werner to confess: 'Je voulais une femme, je n'ai possédé que son cadavre' (p.246). Marital rape will be his futile attempt at conjugal voodoo.

Frantz

I have saved Frantz up for the last, both because he is the last of the leading characters to appear on stage, thus creating suspense, and also because he is the hardest of them all to read legibly. As neither he, his brother nor his sister has or will have children, Frantz is, besides, the last of the line .

The fact that at different times he utters contradictory things could make him unfathomable, or, in the language of recent jargon, undecidable. He himself would certainly prefer such lack of clear-cut definition, for ambiguity hinders sweeping condemnation. It would suit him, down to the ground. If he were mad he would also escape guilt. Often, he tries to claim schizophrenia, a split between mind (or voice) and body, as here, when Leni attempts to convince him that he will be murdered: 'Moi, je parle. La Mort, c'est mon corps qui s'en charge' (p.134). His tape, like Villiers de l'Isle Adam's servants, can aristocratically do his living for him, be his spokesman. The fact remains that Frantz frequently changes his tune. Which Frantz, at which moment, should we trust, if at all?

Although the play as a whole shows Frantz in sequence, as if he were evolving along a temporal line, he himself wishes to inhabit a timeless realm. Given his insoluble dilemma, he cannot, in fact, truly develop, but only thrash around in a net which is partly of his own weaving; he can only, frenziedly, run on the spot. And yet he would have no dramatic impetus if he did not also undergo some modification as a result of his contact and conflict with his intrusive visitors. Although all divisions of such a tormented soul are artificial, we can distinguish between the self-justifications he makes in the interactive presence of others, and those put forward, via his tapes, when he is ranting solo. The latter, after all, are the face he wants to offer to the wider world beyond his family, and his stance before the verdict of posterity. The final tape-recording is, in effect, Frantz's last will and testament. It is, literally, a postmortem. It is up to us readers/spectators to take the further step of a coroner's inquest, and to investigate the causes, the motives, and the degrees of his guilt and/or innocence.

In a famous scene of Malraux's *La Condition humaine*, the hero Kyo fails to recognize his own voice played back on a record. This is a common occurrence, for we hear ourselves internally more than with our ears. Recordings objectify us. A recording-machine, moreover, will register anything – truth, lying, or raving. It is neutral, amoral. Alluding to the use of the *magnéto* by the French military in Algeria to torture their enemies, Simon underlines this ambiguity: 'Une machine qui a presque le même nom [*magnéto*: *magnétophone*] que la machine à faire parler l'homme, parle au nom de l'homme. Victime, bourreau ou témoin. "Un et un font un", répète la voix humaine' (*27*, p.551). Until worn through, the tapes will rehash what they contain *ad nauseam*, indifferently. They will repeat themselves, as if they had consumed a long-lasting radish. In Sarocchi's view, 'la bande tournante du magnétophone peut figurer le cercle vicieux des signes repliés sur eux-mêmes, des consciences incarcérées pour mieux se nuire' (*26*, p.166). After a burst of his forensic eloquence, Johanna checks Werner: 'Arrête! Tu t'écoutes parler' (p.52). This is true of all the characters in this verbose play, and hugely so of Frantz narcissistically admiring himself in his reflective spools. He loves the sound of his own voice. All the same, Frantz must hope that his tapes will be made public, for, if they are not, who or what are they in aid of? Is he addressing only the crab tribunal of a future century?

Obliquely in *La Nausée* and nakedly in *Les Mots*, Sartre evoked his childhood terrors: a hideous claw emerges from deep waters in order to drag a human down. Sartre interpreted this nightmare as a symbol of his own potential monstrosity (though, as Malraux said, each of us is to ourself a monster that we cherish above all others).[12] In *La Force de l'âge*, Simone de Beauvoir relates how in the 1930s Sartre tried mescalin and experienced horrifying hallucinations, in which he was attacked by an octopus and haunted by crabs. Doctors told Sartre that the drug could not have produced of itself these particular hallucinations; they must

---

[12] A. Malraux, *La Condition humaine* (Gallimard, 1946), p. 46.

have been lurking in his subconscious.[13] Still with seafood, Frantz's preferred diet, washed down with champagne, is oysters. Is he symbolically liquidating his hard-shelled accusers? More to the point, where does he imagine oysters and bubbly come from in a supposedly third-world Germany? His complaint (in both senses) has a luxury accompaniment.

Crabs are a truly obsessive image in Sartre's work. Like rooms, hell, or prisons, they are closed, armoured spaces. A shell protects, but also isolates. It is secreted, extruded from inside the beast. Picking up on the French idiom, 'panier de crabes', used to describe people at each other's throats, Sartre likened the French Parliament, in *L'Express* of 25 September 1958, to 'des crabes grouillants, gluants, grimpant sans cesse les uns sur les autres et retombant sans cesse [...] N'est-ce pas une absurdité de soumettre l'homme aux caprices des crabes?' And yet, perversely, that is precisely what he does in *Les Séquestrés d'Altona*, where Frantz visualizes humankind, in the thirtieth century, reduced to unblinking eyes (the Medusa in another guise) and to impervious shells. Lest we forget, the crabs are also us, the audience. Sartre appeals to us as in a law-court, but our tribunal might also be stony-hearted, coldly fish-eyed. In an in-joke between Sartre and his public, Frantz complains at one point: 'Je fais la putain pour leur plaire et ils ne m'écoutent même pas' (p.251). As well as accentuating the idea of judgment, for they are implacable, crabs are self-evidently a-human. This is no doubt why Frantz has locked on to them, for he wishes to evade condemnation by his own species. All in all, the crabs' significance in this play is multiple, but also perhaps meaningless, or inaccessibly psychotic. At one point, Frantz says: 'Ils ne comprennent rien' (p.140). Is his appeal to them deliberately self-defeating?

In his first recorded speech to the crab tribunal, he enters a plea of innocence. He compares his century to a vast clearance-sale (*braderie*), and in a black pun claims that 'la *liquidation* de l'espèce humaine y fut décidée en haut lieu' (p.126, my italics). His speech is self-dramatizing ('je suis votre martyr', p.140), and indeed

---

[13] S. de Beauvoir, *La Force de l'âge* (Gallimard, 1961), pp. 216-17, 228.

megalomaniac. 'Un seul dit vrai: le Titan fracassé, témoin oculaire, séculaire, régulier, séculier, *in secula seculorum*. Moi' (p.126). Read this aloud. These verbal clangs and twists are a sign of word-drunkenness. Listening to this tape a little later, Frantz confesses to Leni: 'Je n'ai pas voulu dire cela. Mais qui parle? Pas un mot de vrai' (p.128). This attempt to cancel himself out could betoken a divided self, schizophrenia, and it marks Frantz out as an unreliable, rather than a definitively false, witness. He is not a consistent liar, and so is even harder to wrongfoot. As at the end of *Huis clos*, 'Tout est à recommencer' (p.128). He hopes that one day he will get the script right. 'Un jour les mots me viendront d'eux-mêmes et je dirai ce que je veux' (p.128). This is a dangerous hope: words spilling out could be garbage, a mental breakdown; his mind's joined-up writing could collapse (as with Pierre in 'La Chambre'). Thus possibility is ever-present. Already, he says to Leni about his speeches to the crabs, 'il m'arrive de dire *blanc* quand je veux leur faire entendre *noir*' (p.139).

The second tape (pp.152 ff.) is even more disconnected, a pickled harangue. During it he hurls oyster-shells at the portrait of Hitler, in one of his many fits of petulance. In the third speech, still talking in global terms, he categorizes the twentieth as the black-sheep century. The theme of counter-finality resurfaces here: 'Le Mal, c'était l'unique matériau. On le travaillait dans nos raffineries. Le Bien, c'était le produit fini. Résultat: le Bien tournait mal. Et n'allez pas croire que le Mal tournait bien' (p.157). This criss-crossing, excruciating conceit marries the ethical and the politico-economic preoccupations of the play. The twentieth century refines not only oil or sugar, but also produces evil in a process that is both deliberate and out of control. In further speeches, he refers to the H-Bomb: the world could be annihilated (p.251). By that stage in the play, Johanna's advent has reintroduced time (she gives him a watch). More importantly, under her impact he offers to sign off the crabs and leave judgment to Johanna. When he says (p.281): 'Je suis tout homme et tout l'Homme, je suis le Siècle (*brusque humilité bouffonne*), comme n'importe qui', he seems to be clownishly veering between the common man and superman. As he has long since renounced straightforwardness, such grim playfulness is as likely to be honest as anything else he utters. I will reserve for later his climactic speech to the crabs.

What emerges from these speeches is Frantz's haughty, all-or-nothing attitude. As he says to Johanna: 'Je ne suis pas du siècle. Je sauverai tout le monde à la fois mais je n'aide personne en particulier' (p.165). To Leni: 'J'écris l'Histoire et tu viens me déranger avec tes anecdotes' (p.131). In such words Frantz sounds like the archetypal French absolutist intellectual dismissing Anglo-Saxon common-sense. Frantz is in fact in awe of History, which for him appears to have replaced God. 'Tout se tient. L'Histoire est une parole sacrée; si tu changes une virgule, il ne reste plus rien' (p.136). This would seem to indicate a manic respect for the facts which the truth-bending Frantz clearly does not possess. In a variant on the Crab tribunal, or the tradition of the Recording Angel, he pictures a black pane. 'Ultrasensible. Un souffle s'y inscrit. Le *moindre* souffle. Toute l'Histoire y est gravée, depuis le commencement du temps jusqu'à ce claquement de doigts' (p.137). The source of this science-fiction vision was a documentary, *Paris 1900*, which Sartre reported on in *Le Figaro* of 25 October 1947. Here Sartre himself was the tribunal of posterity for the era on show. 'Ces existences anonymes et quasiment interchangeables, choisies au hasard par la caméra, répondent devant la postérité pour toute leur époque dont ils sont responsables dans la mesure où ils ont contribué à la faire' (*28*, p.204). Garcin dreaded becoming public property after his death, and no longer having a say in self-defence. Via his tapes, Frantz wishes to go on speaking up for himself, posthumously. He has not totally thrown in the towel. Engels defined good, non-propagandistic literature as a 'delayed-action bomb'.[14] If, as Frantz eventually acknowledges, he achieves little or nothing in his lifetime, he hopes at least to have an effect on us from beyond the grave, in a comparably postponed way.

As with Genet (Sartre's version), the lies and evasions of Frantz help to convey a special truth, which will, Sartre hoped,

---

[14] See P. Demetz, *Marx, Engels and the Poets* (Chicago: Chicago University Press, 1967), pp. 129-30.

home in on the largely bourgeois recipients (a thief needs a receiver), and convince them of their equivalent bad faith. Frantz is himself, of course, often in reeking bad faith. He says to Johanna: 'Mais je ne choisis jamais, ma pauvre amie! Je suis choisi. Neuf mois avant ma naissance, on a fait choix de mon nom, de mon office, de mon caractère et de mon destin' (pp.177-78). Sometimes, he cannot resist pointless quibbling, as when he picks up the cannibal motif from the speech of the crippled woman: 'Et je serais un cannibale? Permettez: tout au plus un végétarien' (p.311). This is an unserious way to refer to torture. His goals are backward-turned, despite the future tribunal. If he could divest himself of guilt, what would he do with himself? Causes, here, are far weightier than objectives. In 1960, Sartre defined bourgeois theatre as concentrating on causes, psychological explanations, and neglecting the pursuit of ends (5, p.124).

Frantz tries desperately to cling to the belief that 'Il fallait la gagner, cette guerre. Par tous les moyens' (p.181). If this were tenable, his torturing might be justified, decriminalized. Yet if he thinks Germany is still in ruins, would this condition not nullify the all-out, no-holds-barred attempt to win the war? Germany would indeed have had fewer ruins if its armies had capitulated sooner. At the heart of his self-defence crouches a symbolic murder: his mad lie reduces 1959 Germany to 1945 ruins. He needs such a catastrophe to lighten his individual burden of guilt. With Machiavelli he wants to believe that 'when the act accuses, the result excuses,[15] and that is another hopeless hope.

It is a gross over-simplification to maintain that 'la "folie" de Frantz est un délire volontaire et parfaitement lucide' (9, p.65). His spasmodic childishness indicates that he is as much controlled as in control. He refers to the bogyman who might get him ('Si les siècles perdent ma trace, la crique me croque', p.131). He keeps a ruler for rapping knuckles. He scoffs his (chocolate) medals ('Je suis un héros lâche', pp.176-77). Like a child, he pathetically begs Leni not to leave him on his own (p.147). He 'acts the crab', possibly as a way of countering his fear of the crustaceans (p.260). On occasion,

---

[15] Machiavelli, *Discourses*, 1, 9.

he simulates the big bad wolf, as when he tells Johanna: 'On vous étranglerait sous mes yeux sans que je lève un doigt. (*Avec complaisance.*) Je vous dégoûte?' (p.166). He is also, here, punishing himself, for he did exactly that when the rabbi was murdered before his eyes.

Frantz has unmistakable delusions of grandeur. He likens himself to Christ, Samson, the Prodigal Son, the Pied Piper of Hamelin, Aeneas carrying on his shoulders his father Anchises, Atlas bearing the whole world. 'Je porte les siècles' (p.258). In *L'Etre et le Néant*, Sartre had proclaimed: 'L'homme, étant condamné à être libre, porte le poids du monde entier sur ses épaules: il est responsable du monde et de lui-même en tant que manière d'être' (*I*, 639). This Atlas-complex was Sartre's not only as a mature man (and again in *Qu'est-ce que la littérature?* where the committed writer is held to be responsible for everything and everyone), but also already as a child when, alone or in cahoots with his friend Paul Nizan, he appointed himself a Superman and saviour of mankind. In Frantz's extremism, then, skulks both Sartre's 1950s self-laceration and his junior delusions, his 'neurosis', as he calls it in *Les Mots*. This extremism, or absolutism, often takes the shape, in Frantz, of either/or, mutually cancelling polarities on a grand scale: 'Il faut que l'Allemagne crève ou que je sois un criminel de droit commun' (p.359). In clinical schizophrenia, such 'folie des grandeurs' is often twinned with a persecution-complex. Frantz's counter-attack on his century is an attempt to generalize guilt in order to lighten his own share for, as Napoleon recognized, 'les crimes collectifs n'engagent personne'.[16] Three years before *Les Séquestrés d'Altona*, Camus's Clamence in *La Chute* had tried a comparably spreading tactic, as a way too of minimizing personal guilt. Frantz's exclamation '*De Profundis Clamavi*' (p.153) is a sign that Sartre and Camus were yodelling to each other across the chasm of their disagreements (*La Chute* reacting against *Saint Genet*, and *Les Séquestrés* against *La Chute*). Genet, like Baudelaire and Flaubert, in Sartre's version of them, is, like Frantz, an enforced hyperbolist. Frantz exacerbates his already terrible position, piles it

---

[16] Napoleon, *Maximes et pensées*, no. 13.

on thick. Playing Mine Own Executioner might spare you being stabbed in the back. On a more down-to-earth level, like the stereotypical Jewish mother of vaudeville, Frantz overcompensates manically.

Do all these symptoms add up to madness, self-chosen or otherwise? Maybe Frantz is not mad enough – to be deemed irresponsible. When he protests to Leni: 'Tu me rendras fou! fou! fou!' she responds: 'Tu le voudrais bien' (p.146). Sartre believed that we choose our psychoses, which is true to the extent that a psychosis is a bipartite attempt to flee and yet to cope. This would remain, however, a 'magical' solution to dilemmas. In his aversion from Freud's doctrine of the unconscious, Sartre refused to let humans off the hook of responsibility. The split stage in *Les Séquestrés* might be taken to suggest schizophrenia, except that the 'ordinary' world downstairs is no less riddled with lies and guilt than the special upstairs universe of Frantz. Perversely, Leni in fact states: 'Elle est là-haut, la vérité' (p.101). Sartre's view of human freedom certainly leaves room for lying, heroic gainsaying. At the very least, such heroic lying is not satisfied with half-measures; and its appeal for the dramatist is self-evident. Alienation, furthermore, signifies both being removed from reality (either through lying or madness) and robbery (in a capitalist world, workers seen as largely robbed of the fruits of their labours and rendered thinglike by the machines they serve).

People not only undergo alienation, but also impart it. Torture is the terminus of all power-urges. One argument would see torture, like war, as beyond traditional morality, a trap-situation in which nobody can be held definitively right or wrong. For Contat, Johanna's reaction of horror at the revelation of Frantz's torturing of prisoners represents that of tender-hearted liberals ('belles âmes'), who decry torture without attacking its cause (in Algeria, the colonial war itself) (*9*, p.52). Remarking on the conjunction Frantz/France, Madeleine Fields reminds that the defeated France of 1940 then experienced twenty years of frequent humiliation (Occupation, Indo-China, Algeria): a fertile breeding-ground for revenge (*11*, p.626). *Les Mains sales* had already underlined the impossibility of keeping clean hands in many concrete situations. In all this, Sartre is not relativist, nor cynical, but anguished. Frantz wanted to be a moral person, but failed. Now he is a war-criminal.

Ideally, if we find Frantz horrifying, it should be, in Sartre's view, because he allowed himself to be programmed by his father (impunity is as bad as guilt), rather than because of the end-product of this conditioning: torture. The fact remains that people are probably more repelled by physical excess than by ethical horrors such as the abdication of responsibility. Moreover, Frantz is not alone. As in *Huis clos*, all of the protagonists torture each other, verbally of course, but words are also sadistic instruments. Torture, conversely, is a brutal form of writing: an inscription of one will on the flesh of another. When Frantz says to Johanna that action is writing one's name and she asks: on what? he replies: 'Sur ce qui se trouve là' (p.304). His victim was indeed a blank page on which Frantz etched his own decision.

The torture on the Eastern Front was set up at home. The Father's truthful jibe, that Frantz does not love underdogs, recalls Hoederer telling Hugo, or Roquentin the Autodidact, that he loves people only in the abstract. Frantz in fact admits to finding unappetizing the inmates of the camp built on his father's land (p.72). The brutal liquidation of the rabbi affords Frantz the luxury of moral indignation not backed up by action. The son was clearly exploiting the Jew, while ostensibly sheltering him, in order to atone for his father's complicity with the Nazis. 'Petit puritain', sneers the Father (p.75). Before Russia, Frantz thus has a moment of choice. It ends in impotence. His act of rescue had been a mere symbolic gesture. The borderline between acts and gestures obsessed Sartre throughout his life, as it must all writers whose interventions in public life are mainly verbal, and so often unavailing. Was Frantz's ultimate torturing a gesture or an act? If a gesture, his chance of free choice evaporates. If it was a true act, he at least fully willed something for once in his life, however disastrously or obscenely or futilely it turned out.

Behind his act lies Sartre's preface to *La Question* by Henri Alleg, who was arrested and tortured by French paratroops in 1957.

There Sartre defined torture as the attempt by one man to turn another into vermin while he was still alive. Also possibly behind Frantz, argues Contat, was the case of Eatherly, who dropped the atomic bomb on Hiroshima, was erected into a hero, but was led by remorse for his act to flee into criminality, as if to demonstrate the sliding overlap between military heroism and moral abjection (9, p.74). A third framing factor is the dominant theme of *Critique de la raison dialectique*: scarcity. While Frantz obviously has never suffered from material shortages, he had since childhood been deprived of sufficient reality, and this is no luxury lack. Unreality, as with Hugo in *Les Mains sales*, was his daily bread. How did this come about?

Frantz's frequent changes of tune betoken his feelings of guilt. He swivels between claiming that the times were to blame; that both Germany and hence himself were innocent victims, after the war, of hyperbolic, hypocritical Allied vengefulness. Later, he argues, no-one is guilty because everyone is. In between these oscillations, for a time he tries to bargain with Johanna to obtain her human forgiveness. At the climax of the play, it is his confrontation with his father that will bring all these matters to a head.

In Act 5, Frantz emerges from his den or bunker at last for the long-postponed face-to-face with his father. This is the first time that Frantz admits he used torture. Immediately he rounds on his interlocutor: 'Je suis tortionnaire parce que vous êtes dénonciateur' (p.341). This sounds essentialist, as if each were fixed into a monotone fate. The only dynamism would come from a dialectic, but this dialogue is one-way, and Frantz did not make his father betray the Jew. In the midst of his self-torturing and counter-accusations, he still feels blood-ties. He feels the pain of his father's cancerous cough: 'Vous me déchirez la gorge' (p.342). He had lacked such empathy in Russia (p.343). For us he relives his past on the Russian Front, where he had the power of life and death over others (his own men as much as enemy prisoners). When he claims that he lived this potentiality up to the hilt, his father reminds him of his powerlessness in the rabbi episode (p.344). For the Father, this experience of impotence set his son off in pursuit of absolute

Les Séquestrés d'Altona

power.

When Frantz calls himself 'la femme de Hitler', he no doubt has in mind the subordinate role (p.345). Even at the time of the rabbi's murder, 'je découvrais, au cœur de mon impuissance, je ne sais quel assentiment'(ibid.). Impotence and connivance were in league with each other. Serving Hitler was a way of escaping himself by becoming Another. 'Hitler m'a fait un Autre, implacable et sacré: lui-même. Je suis Hitler et je me surpasserai' (ibid.). He claims that, if he had not ordered the torture of the Russian partisans, he would have had to helplessly watch it, as with the rabbi (ibid.). 'Je ne retomberai jamais dans l'abjecte impuissance. Je le jure [...] Je revendiquerai le mal, je manifesterai mon pouvoir par la singularité d'un acte inoubliable: changer l'homme en vermine *de son vivant*' (ibid.). This is self-evidently a total inversion of values: an attempt to stamp out, not to affirm, humanity. 'Par un canif et un briquet, je déciderai du règne humain' (p.346). The attempt turned out pointless: the Russian captives died without giving anything away. Ironically, or counter-finally, the prisoners, in the midst of their abjection, defined what being human means: refusing inhumanity. By an equivalent irony, nearly all of Frantz's men, whom he used torture to protect, were themselves killed a few days later. Frantz's supposedly grand act of self-affirmation amounted to an anti-climax.

Frantz admits his monstrous egocentricity. Germany could go to hell as long as he could feel justified in what he had done: 'J'ai souhaité la mort de mon pays' (p.347). The Father refuses to be his son's natural judge, an offer which Frantz makes only after a struggle with himself. Yet another dramatic anti-climax arises when von Gerlach reveals that he has known for three years of the events at Smolensk, from two survivors who came to blackmail, and whom he as usual certainly silenced (p.352). Father and son yield on occasion to emotion – Frantz sobbing in his father's embrace – but the son soon flinches away, an untouchable, like the family in general. Although von Gerlach has changed more over the years than Frantz, who has frozen him in a past, cut-and-dried role, will allow, he undoubtedly clings to his old reflexes, especially that of the would-be fixer of all problems. He is lucid, and indeed very astute on the pain of insentience (what Garcin called 'souffrance de tête'): 'Tu es possédé depuis quatorze ans par une souffrance que tu as fait naître et que tu ne ressens pas' (p.356). Does Frantz indeed suffer not from an excess but from a lack of feelings? Were his victims, because human, his superiors?

Turning the screws ever tighter, the Father forces Frantz's eyes open to 1959 Germany's economic miracle: 'On nous gâte; tous les marchés nous sont ouverts, nos machines tournent: c'est une forge. Défaite providentielle. Frantz: nous avons du beurre et des canons' (p.357). (This last phrase picks up Goering's challenging question in 1936: 'Would you rather have butter or guns?') Von Gerlach claims that he, and those like him, played 'Loser takes all' from the outbreak of hostilities (though how could this be true, when defeat was not then certain?), and that this strategy made all military acts inherently futile, for industrialists thought they would win out, whatever the war's outcome. In effect, the Father is nihilating his son. 'Ta vie, ta mort, de toute façon, c'est *rien*. Tu n'es rien, tu ne fais rien, tu n'as rien fait, tu ne peux rien faire' (p.360). The verdict sounds conclusive.

Von Gerlach, however, wants to confess also to his own delusions. In his scheme of things, the future of the child Frantz was to be simply the Father's past, replayed. In other words, his father wanted to make Frantz a chip off the old block, a spitting image: an Other, but with no separate self, no personal identity. Von Gerlach repeats his earlier admission of his own powerlessness as head of the firm: 'Je possède mais je ne commande plus' (p.361). As a way of possibly retaining at least some semblance of power, he persists in arguing that he takes total responsibility for having constructed Frantz in his own image in order to fit his project. Confusing Father and God the Father, Frantz has indeed made a fetish, a false idol out of von Gerlach and kowtowed before it. After Oreste in *Les Mouches* and Hugo in *Les Mains sales*, who both sought to liquidate their genitors, Frantz recognizes his.

Both Father and son are in impossible positions. Von Gerlach will be dead, anyway, in a few months, and Frantz has little or nothing to live for. Frantz it is who decides on an immediate and joint suicide. In a final attempt at shouldering true responsibility for his own actions, Frantz maintains that he tasted one moment of real independence, at Smolensk: 'Vous êtes coupable de tout sauf de cela' (p.364). And yet the pair end up chorusing the opposite. The father: 'Je t'ai fait, je te déferai'. Frantz: 'Vous aurez été ma cause et mon destin jusqu'au bout' (p.367). Neither von Gerlach nor Frantz will commit suicide out of remorse – always a sterile cop-out in Sartre's relentless eyes – but rather out of a sense of total uselessness. Though, unlike the trio of *Huis clos*, Frantz and his father choose the moment and the manner of their death, it is hard to see this as a free choice, for it is too weightily conditioned by all that has gone before. Frantz will move from being the skeleton in the cupboard to a public corpse.

He has, however, the last word: what he considers his best-scripted recorded speech to the crabs, from six years before (a sure sign that he makes no forward progress, but only, like a crab, reverse or lateral). In it, he accuses both his century and himself: 'Siècles, voici mon siècle, solitaire et difforme, l'accusé' (p.374). The twentieth century, of course, invented neither torture nor genocide, nor even capitalism, yet Frantz wants to single our century out as specially guilty. 'Le siècle eût été bon si l'homme n'eût été guetté par son ennemi cruel, immémorial, par l'espèce carnassière qui avait juré sa perte, par la bête sans poil et maligne, par l'homme' (p.374). The word 'immémorial' should have reminded Sartre that the hairless beast dates back to Adam. In addition, Man is not the only cannibalistic species. Homing in on himself rather than on the species, Frantz faces up to his own bestiality. 'J'ai surpris la bête, j'ai frappé, un homme est tombé, dans ses yeux mourants j'ai vu la bête, toujours vivante, moi' (ibid.). This striking image, in which we are shown as killing in others what we loathe in ourselves, sounds simply true for once. But what of the enigmatic statement: 'Un et un font un, voilà notre mystère'? (ibid.). Good beings and evil beings jointly constitute humankind, in a kind of unholy trinity? In Act 1, when Frantz relives his concealment of the rabbi, he says to his father: 'C'est pour vous.

Vous, c'est moi' (p.80). In *Morts sans sépulture* (1946), the tortured martyrs of the Resistance support each other by mutual esteem: 'Nous ne faisons qu'un'. Frantz and his father reach the same formulation at the end, but it is turned inside-out. All that they share is impotence, emptiness, not reciprocal respect. Earlier, had claimed of his father: 'Je le connais comme si je l'avais fait. Et, pour tout dire, je ne sais plus trop qui de nos deux a fait l'autre' (p.169). There is some truth in this. Von Gerlach has lived through his son, and is in effect his son's prisoner, dependent on the sound of Frantz's footfalls. They share insomnias. Listening from below to his son's restless pacing, von Gerlach pathetically says: 'C'est une manière d'être ensemble' (p.111). The lines of Robert Graves on lovers come to mind: 'After, when they disentwine/You from me and yours from mine,/Neither can be certain who/ Was that I whose mine was you'.[17] As Frantz says, parodying yet again Holy Writ: 'Il m'a créé à son image – à moins qu'il ne soit devenu l'image de ce qu'il créait' (p.160). This sounds curiously and fittingly like the fate of workers under capitalism, who sign away their own substance into what they produce.

Father and son zoom off in a powerful sports car towards the Devil's Bridge. All that is left of Frantz for us is his still defiant voice on an empty stage, as the spool winds on. The last words end with his manic tic. 'Moi, Frantz, von Gerlach, ici, dans cette chambre, j'ai pris le siècle sur mes épaules et j'ai dit: j'en répondrai. En ce jour et pour toujours. Hein quoi?' (p.375). But is he Christ, taking the load off our shoulders? Surely the idea of representative suffering is much too Christian for the atheist Sartre?

It seems rather facile to say, like Contat: 'Si Frantz est un personnage ambigu, haïssable et pourtant fraternel, c'est qu'il incarne à l'excès les ambiguïtés de notre époque et de notre société' (*9*, p.67). Frantz's sense of a mission – to save himself, Germany and mankind before the tribunal of posterity – seems to repeat the child of *Les Mots*, convinced that he must fulfil expectations, be mandated, for otherwise he would feel (and did feel) superfluous, an

---

[17] R. Graves, 'Lovers', *Selected Poems* (Harmondsworth: Penguin, 1986), pp. 142-43.

unnecessary addition to humanity. Frantz's final speech of accusation against himself and his fellow creatures moves beyond this Superman urge, to recognize a common humanity, and a common bestiality. Frantz is not, like the Sartre of *Les Mots* or of a lifetime career, a writer, so that 'solution' to his impasse is not available to him. His only writing was on the flesh of his victims. But he does record his version. This fact scarcely injects optimism, for instance that of *Les Mouches*: 'La vie humaine commence de l'autre côté du désespoir' (p.238). Frantz is left mainly with the style of his recognition. In this he continues the trio of *Huis clos*, for he is no less the walking dead than they. It is by the quality of his lucidity and of his rhetoric that he reaches, if at all, the level of Greek, French Classical or Shakespearean tragic heroes. Indeed, he is Shakespearean in his strong buffoonish tendencies. For Louette, *Les Séquestrés d'Altona* is one of Sartre's 'tragédies-bouffes' (*19*, p.141).

Black Comedy

Black comedy excruciates, and is thus a variant torture, as it was before in *Huis clos*. As well as its overt statements, a play's collective or piecemeal tone dictates its impact on us. *Les Séquestrés d'Altona* deals in extreme, terminal situations, and the German term *Galgenhumor* (gallows-humour) seems peculiarly apt for much of its action (cf. the manic giggling that comes over some people in desperate situations). Sartre always resisted 'l'esprit de sérieux', which he held responsible for leading people into bad faith. Such resistance suggests a countervailing ludism, but always a *pointed* playfulness. Early in the play, von Gerlach refers to his cancer as 'Une mort industrielle' (p.25). He and Frantz will die from a different 'industrial death' in a self-willed car-crash.

Puns are a notorious branch of excruciation. The clichéic reaction to them is to wince or grimace at the collision of meanings engineered in wordplay. 'Cancer' is a supreme example. It refers also to crabs. Frantz's neuroses have lodged in his father's throat. Obsession with Frantz helps to kill von Gerlach just as his son's fixation on his father leaves nowhere but death to fly to. Offering her brother another tape, Leni says: 'Qu'est-ce que tu veux, maître chanteur?' (p.127). A Meistersinger suits perfectly the Wagnerian echoes, indeed ethos at times, of this apocalyptic play; and Frantz, like all of the players in turn, is the other kind of 'maître chanteur': an (emotional) blackmailer. The crippled woman crouching by the wall in Frantz's 'dream' moves from the literal 'Je suis au pied du mur' to the punning literalization: 'J'ai mis au pied du mur un soldat de chez nous' (p.289). Back to the wall is a favoured stance of the aggressive/defensive punner.

The image of the tourniquet, much favoured by Sartre in his massive study of Flaubert's 'neurosis', and which centres on excruciation of attitudes and language, operates again in this play: the tourniquet is a painful antidote to pain (and in military slang means a court-martial). Sartre's honesty makes him see the funny side of everything. Johanna says to von Gerlach: 'Tout est comique, au rez-de-chaussée, même vous qui allez mourir' (p.217). As the other kind of *comédie*, play-acting, develops between her and Frantz upstairs also, she could extend her mockery to the whole house. Striving to deny her impact on him, Frantz says: 'La chambre a reçu le vide en coup de faux' (p.166). This could mean either that her essential emptiness scythed into the room, like Death; or that something counterfeit (*faux*) has emptied the room of meaning. Neither possibility flatters her.

Punning superimposes. As a would-be absolutist, Frantz necessarily exaggerates. He lifts up to hyperbolic levels what Sartre sees as a universal human ability, or disability: we are all, always, in danger of not acting but play-acting. As Howells says: 'Sartre uses the inherent insubstantiality of the theatrical medium both to embody and to denounce play-acting' (*15*, p.75). In other words, Sartre uses the device of self-referentiality (as in Frantz's in-joke with the audience) less to break the theatrical spell, which he values highly, than to underline the inescapable link, for him, of living and *comédie*. Sartre can be taken as a hyperbolist himself, as when he inflates our freedom of choice. Even in dreaming can we be totally free? The commonest refrain of Sartre's many enemies over the years is that, however insightful in places, he generalizes and exaggerates overall. His defence would be the one he furnished for Genet: 'Il faut écouter la voix de Genet notre prochain, notre frère [...] il enfle nos sophismes jusqu'à les faire éclater [...] il exagère notre mauvaise foi jusqu'à nous la rendre intolérable, il fait paraître au grand jour notre culpabilité'.[18] This does not answer the charge; it dismisses it, and counter-attacks.

The general mood and tone of the play is that of exacerbation. Far more acutely than in Anouilh's 'pièces grinçantes', people here grate on each other's nerve-ends; on top of this Frantz grinds his oyster-shells together. Logorrhea alternates with suppression. A family living largely in isolation from the outside world, living or wanting to live in each other's pockets (cf. the incest-motif), can pick up allusions, hints, and can chime in with echo-effects. Yet despite the loquacity and the smartness, nobody speaks straight; all have ulterior motives. The go-between Leni, requested to report on Frantz, says that 'Là-haut, les mots n'ont pas le même sens [...] En quelle langue? Il faut tout le temps traduire' (pp.220-21).

At times, the dialogue falls into that *marivaudage* that Marivaux himself generally avoided; verbal conceits, excessively clever points-scoring. When Johanna calls Frantz's madness her cage as well, he responds, preciously: 'Vous tournez, petit écureuil? Les écureuils ont de bonnes dents: vous rongerez les barreaux' (p.277). He will, he swears, renounce his delusion, 'Quand je vous aimerai plus que mes mensonges, quand vous m'aimerez malgré ma vérité' (p.279). That is: when pigs might fly, for he has always known that blowing the gaff on his torture will alienate Johanna from him irrevocably. Frantz has, however, the courage of his excruciation. He debonairly purloins Henri IV's historic words ('Paris vaut bien une messe', when he converted to Catholicism for reasons of state): 'L'Allemagne vaut bien un crime, hein, quoi?' (p.311).

Delusions, naturally, distort even sight. Like the tape-machine, eyes do not invariably register the truth, any more than a camera cannot lie. Frantz admits as much: 'Avec ces mêmes yeux, il

---

[18] Sartre, *Saint Genet* (Gallimard, 1952), p. 549.

nous arrivait de voir ce qui n'existe pas' (p.166). Hitler had been his mirage; Frantz had seen in him what he wanted to see: a saviour, a guarantor of Frantz's weak reality. The gaze, in *Les Séquestrés d'Altona* as in *Huis clos*, functions powerfully. Frantz complains to Leni: 'Tu me regardes: la nuque me brûle' (p.145). The nape is the most vulnerable part of our anatomy to another's stare, as we cannot ourselves see it but only feel the gaze boring into our defenceless flesh. People can of course turn the tables. The gaze can be imagined detached from us, hovering above others, as when, in a paroxysm of sexual jealousy, Frantz pictures Werner crushing Johanna beneath him. Frantz says to her, sadistically: 'Cette nuit, quand il vous prendra, vous saurez que je veille' (p.264). It is as though merely keeping the eyes open could act as a distant surveillance. Everybody, besides, in this play spies on everyone else (Leni to father: 'Je vous épiais. Chacun son tour', p.208). Frantz: 'Nous vivons en résidence surveillée [...] Toi, moi, tous ces morts: les hommes' (p.137). He utters this facing the audience. We are all included; the theatre becomes a police-state. As always, the gaze is judgment. When Johanna recoils in horror from him, Frantz exclaims: 'Pas ces yeux! Non. Pas ces yeux-là!' (p.332). To armour himself, he at once goes into his crab-routine.

What of the audience's, the readers' eyes? The actors on the stage, or the black marks on the white page, certainly do not exist properly until they are seen in the flesh, in the mind's eye, or scanned on the page. We readers/spectators are meant to stand in, to be a microcosm, for society at large. Our eyes objectify and judge the people and events on stage.

Distancing

The black comedy helps to distance Frantz and his family, making it both easier to condemn them and harder to sympathize with them. Sartre used the distancing afforded by classical mythology in *Les Mouches*, by the extraterrestrial setting in *Huis clos*, by history in *Le Diable et le Bon Dieu*. In *Les Séquestrés d'Altona*, he resorted to geographical displacement. This would help, he believed, to produce his desired effect: 'J'aimerais que le public voie, du dehors, notre siècle, chose étrangère, en témoin. Et qu'en même temps il participe, puisqu'il fait ce siècle. Il y a d'ailleurs quelque chose de particulier à notre époque: c'est que nous savons que nous serons jugés' (*5*, p.103). Two millennia of Christianity scooped Sartre. It is clear from this statement that distancing does not rule out involvement. It can accentuate it, just as understatement can emphasize. Sartre sounds often like Brecht in this respect. Indeed, Sartre saluted in Brecht his rejection of bourgeois theatre and its tradition of encouraging audience identification with its characters. 'L'idéal du théâtre brechtien, ce serait que le public fût comme un groupe d'ethnographes rencontrant tout à coup une peuplade sauvage. S'approchant et se disant soudain, dans la stupeur: ces sauvages, c'est nous' (*5*, p.101).

Brecht, however, remained, in Sartre's view, too much of an orthodox Marxist, too dogmatic, and his theory of *Verfremdungseffekt* (alienation-effect) too rationalistic, dehumanized and overexplanatory. As Roubine picturesquely puts it, Sartre performed a 'hesitation-waltz' with Brecht (*25*, p.998). Sartre himself was always torn between appealing to the freedom of the receiver and seeking to control it. Besides, Sartre believed that Brecht's German audiences were already politicized, whereas French audiences needed to be deconditioned from their prejudice against politics on stage, before a dramatist could hope to inflect their opinions. Always ready to accept that art proposes a lie, a generous lie, Sartre saw his job in this area in these terms: 'Je crois, moi, profondément, que toute démystification doit être en un sens mystifiante. Ou plutôt que, devant une foule en partie mystifiée, on ne peut se fier aux seules réactions critiques de cette foule. Il faut lui fournir une contre-mystification, et pour cela le théâtre ne doit se priver d'aucune des sorcelleries du théâtre' (*5*, p.77). Of Protestant descent, Sartre would act the Jesuit 'pour les besoins de la cause', and, like Goetz in *Le Diable et le Bon Dieu*, lie, heroically, to the troops. Brecht, besides, though apparently trusting his audience to have the politically correct reactions, engineers these just as surely as any other playwright. On stage, as elsewhere, facts rarely speak for themselves. Both writers reconverge in wanting their spectators to refuse any claim to inevitability made on stage; the audience should be persuaded that change is possible. Though little change seems available to the protagonists of *Les Séquestrés d'Altona* throughout it or at the end, such ruined lives, such half-lives, may still have awful, cautionary value. Who would want to emulate any of them? Sartre had little optimism left at the time of this play, only critical realism. 'Si un héros, à la fin, se réconcilie avec lui-même, le public qui le regarde faire – dans la pièce – risque de se réconcilier avec ses interrogations, avec les questions non résolues' (*4*, p.328). An unsatisfying, non-resolved Frantz might thus stir his watchers to dissatisfaction with themselves and their society. [19]

Structure

'Mes pièces [...] m'ont presque toutes échappé. Elles deviennent des objets [...] Le théâtre est tellement *la chose publique, la chose du public*' (*5*, p.93). Sartre's admission here is less humility or a sop to audience vanity than simple realism. This is one distancing that the medium itself imposes. Within a play, though Sartre tries to give a fair crack of the whip to 1960s-style theatrical 'happenings', where actors mingled with audiences or dragged spectators on stage, he was clearly uneasy at the abolition of the imaginary and of distancing (*5*, p.180). He approved, however, of the play-within-the-play (as in *Hamlet*), for this was distance squared ('au second degré', *5*, p.29). In *Les Séquestrés d'Altona*, flashbacks (and the tape-recorder) fulfil this role.

This is not quite the aptest term: rather, re-enactments (Sartre calls them 'scènes-souvenirs'). In the stage-directions, he writes: '*Le ton et le jeu des personnages qui jouent une scène-souvenir doivent comporter une sorte de recul, de "distanciation" qui, même dans la violence, distingue le passé du présent*' (p.62). Such scenes in fact shuttle between past and present. The fact that the past often seems more real than the present embodies Sartre's conviction that

---

[19] Sartre, besides, is notorious for his unfinished projects (*Les Chemins de la liberté*, *Mallarmé*, *L'Idiot de la famille*, etc.).

Les Séquestrés d'Altona

no such facile boundaries are admissible, for they are too easily used as pretexts ('That was then; this is now'). In addition to being a dead weight, the past can come alive.

In the first of such scenes, the Father is more on trial than his son, for he is trying to shuffle out of the responsibility for colluding with the Nazis (p.67). Of course it suits both of them in this scene to widen the onus of responsibility beyond themselves. Frantz spins round the apportioning of guilt towards the Allies, who dropped the atomic bomb on Hiroshima. He has a valid point, but characteristically belabours it by accusing the Allies of trying to exterminate systematically the entire German people. In his view, all (Father, son, Goering, the Germans) are innocent (p.70).

The scenes with the Feldwebel and the crippled old woman are described as dreams (see pp.156, 295). On the other hand, the scenes on the Eastern Front, featuring Frantz and Lt. Klages, are highly dynamic, because the moment of truth is fast approaching, and Frantz shuttles rapidly between the evoked past and his present with Johanna (p.303). Klages (the name suggests 'bemoaning') is the idealistic son of a Protestant pastor, who seeks to keep his hands spotless in a filthy situation. He and Frantz argue over the question of military discipline, the giving and obeying of orders, which is obviously of vital concern to the obedient son/commanding officer Frantz (p.301). Even in flashbacks, Frantz continues play-acting, as the big bad wolf, the bullying Nazi officer, towards his inferior Heinrich ('Tu réponds, sac à merde?', p.307). He likens Klages to Jesuits on the score of 'mental reservations'. Not unlike the father, Klages 'condamnait les nazis dans son âme pour se cacher qu'il les servait dans son corps' (p.303).

In the main body of the play, the theme of *comédie* recurs frequently. The Father describes the ex-actress Johanna in these terms: 'Ce sont des menaces de théâtre: le dépit a ressuscité l'actrice et l'actrice a voulu sa sortie' (p.99). Thus does he try to rob her of seriousness. Frantz 'acts the crab', or goose-steps (p.146). Everybody is putting on an act, while desperate for the truth. Stage-directions at times stress that a look, a tone of voice, a set of words, are to be played ambiguously, so that the receiver does not know whether they are genuine or ironic (see p.26). An example: Frantz. '*Avec une inquiétude dont on ne sait pas si elle est sincère ou jouée*' (p.138). Sincerity, besides, is always a riddled concept in Sartre's work, because there remains stuck to it, for him, a strong sense of complacency, whereas true authenticity would depend on a relationship of equality with others, not just on self-satisfaction.

A key element of structure in most plays is suspense. The Father's tactics, those of a man obsessed with bosshood, are: make them wait (whether his company board or his children). In their long-postponed face-to-face, Frantz says to his father: 'Je les connais vos longues, longues attentes: j'en ai vu en face de vous, des durs, des méchants. Ils vous injuriaient, vous ne disiez rien, vous attendiez: à la fin les bonshommes se liquéfiaient [turned to jelly] (p.348). This choice is tied up with his seeing himself, like his son, as providential: the awaited saviour. In turn, of course, the mighty Father has been pathetically waiting for many years to see Frantz again, and is now counting the days to his own death from cancer: the inescapable deadline. At the end, Leni and Johanna perform a countdown as they wait for the ineluctable car-crash. Werner waits in the wings. Leni waits on Frantz hand and foot. Johanna hopes for release, and hovers between Frantz and Werner. Purgatory is also a waiting-room.

Staging

Rooms are indeed crucial to this play, as to *Huis clos* (whether that in Hell or those back on earth). They embody the imprisonment of the title and of the dramas enacted in them. It is strangely appropriate to end this study with the staging, for the last image of the play is of a depopulated stage inhabited only by objects.

Though the staging in both *Huis clos* and *Les Séquestrés d'Altona* is sparser and less eye-catching than in countless naturalistic plays, the physical situation of each play's characters – the hell they inhabit – is crucial. Sartre's plays are never just ideas-plays, *pièces à thèse*. The ideas are grounded, made palpable, given sense by what surrounds them. The downstairs room boasts ugly, late nineteenth-century German furniture, suggesting the time-warp of the 1959 characters. Three large photos of Frantz, draped in black, both liquidate and memorialize him. (Justin O'Brien alone has pointed out that Altona is in fact an industrial sector of Hamburg, near the docks, and so is an unlikely site for a dynast's mansion. O'Brien also would prefer for an English title the punning *The Family Cell*).[20] Frantz's room is in fact a spartan cell – fit for a prisoner, a monk or a madman. He wants to keep in goose-step with a ruined Germany, and so his furniture is ramshackle and his uniform tattered. In addition to the portrait of Hitler, the oyster-shells, champagne-bottles, glasses and a ruler, and the indispensable tape-machine, a few slogans on the walls ('Il est défendu d'avoir peur', 'Don't disturb') complete the accoutrements of the room. By Act 4 this décor is slightly simplified: the mottoes have disappeared. The props, like everything and everyone else in the play, house ambivalence. When Frantz abrades the oyster-shells together, it is unclear whether this is an uncontrollable tic, or simply a way of annoying and silencing the pestering Leni (p.145). Frantz's only other artificial aid, with the champagne he quaffs, is that benzedrine that Sartre also stuffed himself with at the time of writing *Les Séquestrés d'Altona*.

The windows are stopped up: only artificial light burns in this room bolted from the inside. Though he could leave at any time, it takes Frantz four acts of the play to emerge from the trap he has sprung for himself. *Piège* and *pièce* are phonic cousins: all Sartre's plays are mousetraps of a kind undreamt of by Agatha Christie. As in *Huis clos*, the artificial light is that of the third degree, though even harsh light can be an unreliable sign. Johanna speaks of 'la lumière froide des vérités entières et des mensonges parfaits' (p.112). Needing to stay alert in his room as on the Eastern front, Frantz orders: 'Envoyez les phares, vous autres! Plein feu: dans la gueule, au fond des yeux, ça réveille' (p.153). Estelle needed a mirror in order to feel alive. Frantz, who like Inès needs to entertain evil in order to feel alive, wants to be heard as well as to be lit up by

---

[20] J. O'Brien, *The French Literary Horizon* (New Brunswick: Rutgers University Press, 1967), pp. 389, 391.

brutal light: 'Si vous ne m'écoutez pas, je m'endors' (ibid.). This, of course, is one way of keeping a faltering auditorium on its toes, a wise tactic in such a lengthy and exhausting play.

Conclusion

At the suicidal climax, an impatient reader/playgoer might mutter: 'Good riddance to bad rubbish'. Before consigning father, son and the rest, however, to the dustbin of history, we should ask ourselves to what extent they are recyclable. When I emerged from a Liverpool theatre after seeing the English production, I felt not washed out, as in a classical catharis or purgation, but heavily bloated, as if I had ingested a copious meal I would have trouble digesting. The play is anti-Christian. There is no absolution for crimes committed. *La Chute* had already proposed that confession liberates no-one. Clamence lived cabined, cribbed and confined in the *malconfort*, that cell where you can neither stand or lie down, but must endure on the slant. When Frantz talks of our black-sheep century, there is no suggestion that it will ever be welcomed back into the fold.

Les Séquestrés d'Altona is much more in the fatalistic Racinian tradition, to which Sartre usually preferred the voluntaristic Cornelian one. If it seems often a histrionic, shrill play, it is so necessarily. Its family has de-realized itself, become (like the family thespians of *Les Mots*) a repertory-company. As Sarocchi puts it: 'Ainsi, dans *Les Séquestrés*, le cauchemar des consciences, s'exténue-t-il en un jeu grinçant et pipé [...] Mais comment s'étonner qu'une œuvre centrée sur la traîtrise ne bascule dans le truquage, et ne désintègre ses virtualités tragiques en effets de comédie' (*26*, p.171). Beneath all the bandages of sophistication, raw wounds leak. Sartre puts his characters and his audiences on the spot.

Even critics favourable to Sartre often complain that his theatre is too much talk and too little show. Yet this imbalance may be the play's deepest theme. As well as being victims of history, in hock to our past, dependent on others, we are above all a prey to words. For corporeal beings, we are astoundingly abstract and word-dominated. And so the final scene – a tape-recorder ranting to a deserted stage – is a telling image of the human condition, seen in the bleakest light. We use words, desperately, to keep at bay horror, madness, reality. (We also use them to befriend, love, console and joke, but a play cannot be a whole picture.)

Several French reviewers claimed confidently – but how could they know? – that the audiences of this play came out unchanged, uncomprehending, not seeing the Germany/France connexion which Sartre had smuggled in. For Gisselbrecht, 'l'illusion d'avoir pensé un moment par procuration' is the most that Sartre's middle-class audiences can have experienced. As for Sartre himself, the height of his achievement was mere morose delectation (*13*, pp.126 and 107). As Champigny noted wryly, if this play did have political impact, it was hardly of the kind Sartre relished. The recall of the loathed de Gaulle to resolve the Algerian dilemma was a superb instance of history's counter-finality, or dramatic irony (*8*, p.99). This can hardly have been what Sartre had in mind when he remarked to Tynan: 'It has been said that progress is made laterally, in a sideways motion, rather like the movement of crabs' (*30*, p.304).

When the play was restaged in 1965, Sartre wrote in the programme that, because the question of French torture in Algeria was, since independence, no longer relevant, the play's leading question became the more general, and indeed eternal, one: 'Qu'as-tu fait de ta vie?' (*5*, p.358). The poet Villon was already asking this poser five hundred years earlier, as might any human being in any era. We might extend the question. Can we undo what we have done? Furthermore, can we stop others (people, systems) undoing us? In his preface to *Le Traître* by André Gorz (1958), Sartre admitted to having been deeply affected by the book, which made him ask himself questions such as: 'Est-ce que nous *reconnaissons* nos enterprises? Est-ce qu'elles ne deviennent pas *autres* en se réalisant?' The anguished 'traitor' of the book sounds like Frantz *avant la lettre*: 'Un traître; un type lézardé comme nous tous, mais qui ne pouvait plus supporter sa duplicité'. Each of us, however guilty, is 'un unique n'importe qui': a nonpareil anybody (*3(4)*, pp.48, 57, 79).

In *Huis clos* the bourgeoisie and in *Les Séquestrés d'Altona* the merchant class suffer exemplarily. As in *Huis clos*, Sartre here chooses corny examples: the familiar dilemmas of upper bourgeois dynasties. Fernandez lists the stock ingredients. 'Un drame bourgeois, auquel ne manquent ni le *pater familias*, ni le fils raté, ni la fille incestueuse, ni la bru adultère'.[21] Sartre then sets up a startling contrast of partly stereotyped downstairs and over-the-top upstairs, just as in *Huis clos* the ordinariness of the décor accentuates the hellishness of the goings-on. A common reactionary jibe against Sartre has been that this writer obsessed with sequestration was certifiable himself and should be locked away. One main reason why Sartre wrote so often in cafés was to escape the claustrophobia of the writer's lonely room, and to keep people in close view.

Though Sartre was as much of a mind-bender and spin-doctor and jogger of readers' rib-cages as any other writer, his best effort was always to appeal to the potential for freedom in those readers. He lays his work on the line; the rest is up to us.

Like the living dead of *Huis clos*, the sequestered ones act as an awful warning. Yet, whatever their crimes and faults, they are human beings, however reduced their humanity, and no humans are discountable, or else we end up like Frantz condoning or practising torture. In 'la bête humaine' are two unblinkable realities: the beast and humankind, the human beast. This play shows our century, our society, as in many ways suicidal, bent on our own destruction. So the wretched pair at the end are flamboyantly enacting a global dilemma. Mauriac's description of Sartre as 'incurably harmless' is arrant nonsense.[22]

If I have, despite my efforts, presented too frozen an image of Sartre, I would recommend these true, corrective words from the American novelist and essayist, William Gass. 'Sartre, at his deepest point, is anarchistic, playful, ironic, proud, lonely, detached,

---

[21] D. Fernandez, '*Les Séquestrés d'Altona*', *NRF*, 83 (1 Nov. 1959), 896.

[22] F. Mauriac, quoted in *The Times*, 30 June 1970.

superior, unique. It is a painful position and it is not surprising that the surface flow of his life and his thinking should run so strongly in the direction of humorless moralizing and the obliteration of the self.'[23] I would add that in *Huis clos* and *Les Séquestrés d'Altona* he comes close to melding the two tensions described above. Despite his often obtuse dogmatism, Sartre always dreaded seeming to be comfortably in the right – the distinguishing mark of *salauds* infected with *l'esprit de sérieux*.

I could do worse than end with these lines of Queneau, pointed at all writers, and readers:

> Les voilà tous qui s'imaginent
> que dans cette vaste combine
> ils agissent tous comme ils le veulent
> comme s'ils savaient ce qu'ils voulaient
> comme s'ils voulaient ce qu'ils voulaient
> comme s'ils voulaient ce qu'ils savaient
> comme s'ils savaient ce qu'ils savaient.[24]

---

[23] W. Gass, *The World within the Word* (New York: Knopf, 1978), p. 196.

[24] R. Queneau, 'Chêne et chien', *Œuvres complètes*, vol. 1 (Gallimard, 1989), p. 21.

Bibliography

Place of publication is Paris, unless otherwise stated. I have confined the bibliography to books and articles directly useful for an understanding of the two plays.

WORKS BY SARTRE

1. *L'Etre et le Néant* (Gallimard, 1943)
2. *Critique de la raison dialectique* (Gallimard, 1960)
3. *Situations*, vols 1-10 (Gallimard, 1947-1976). (The volume quoted from is in the style *3(3)*.)
4. *Les Ecrits de Sartre*, edited by Michel Contat and Michel Rybalka (Gallimard, 1970)
5. *Un Théâtre de situations*, edited by Michel Contat and Michel Rybalka (Gallimard, 1973)

BOOKS AND ARTICLES ON SARTRE

6. Barnes, Hazel, *Sartre* (London, Quartet, 1974)
7. Boros, Marie-Denise, *Un Séquestré: l'homme sartrien* (Nizet, 1968)
8. Champigny, Robert, *Sartre and Drama* (York, S.C.: French Literature Publications, 1982)
9. Contat, Michel, *Explication des Séquestrés d'Altona* (Minard, 1968)
10. Cranston, Maurice, *Sartre* (Edinburgh: Oliver and Boyd, 1962)
11. Fields, Madeleine, 'De *La Critique de la raison dialectique* aux *Séquestrés d'Altona*', PMLA, 78 (1963), 622-30
12. Galster, Ingrid, *Le Théâtre de Jean-Paul Sartre devant ses premiers critiques* (Tübingen/Paris: Narr/J-M. Place, 1986)
13. Gisselbrecht, André, 'A propos des *Séquestrés d'Altona*', *La Nouvelle Critique*, 111 (1959), 119 ff., and 114 (1960), 101-19
14. Goldthorpe, Rhiannon, *Sartre: Literature and Theory* (Cambridge: Cambridge University Press, 1984)
15. Howells, Christina, *Sartre: The Necessity of Freedom* (Cambridge: Cambridge University Press, 1988)
16. Lecherbonnier, Bernard, '*Huis clos*': *Sartre* (Hatier, 1972)
17. Lorris, Robert, *Sartre dramaturge* (Nizet, 1975)

Bibliography

18. Louette, Jean-François, 'L'Expression de la folie dans *Les Séquestrés d'Altona*', *Les Temps Modernes*, 565-66 (1993), 77-132
19. ——, *Jean-Paul Sartre* (Hachette, 1993)
20. McCall, Dorothy, *The Theatre of Jean-Paul Sartre* (New York: Columbia University Press, 1969)
21. Murdoch, Iris, *Sartre* (Cambridge: Bowes and Bowes, 1953)
22. Noudelmann, François, '*Huis clos*' *et* '*Les Mouches*' *de Jean-Paul Sartre* (Gallimard, 1993)
23. Palmer, J.N.J., '*Les Séquestrés d'Altona*: Sartre's black tragedy', *French Studies* 24, 2 (1970), 150-62
24. Pucciani, Oreste, '*Les Séquestrés d'Altona*', in *Sartre: a collection of critical essays*, edited by Edith Kern (Englewood Cliffs, N.J.: Prentice-Hall), pp.92-103
25. Roubine, Jean-Jacques, 'Sartre devant Brecht', *Revue d'Histoire littéraire de la France*, 77, 6 (Nov.-Dec. 1977), 985-1001
26. Sarocchi, Jean, 'Sartre dramaturge: *Les Mouches* et *Les Séquestrés d'Altona*', *Travaux de Linguistique et de Littérature*, 8, 2 (1970), 157-72
27. Simon, André, 'Un et un font un', *Esprit*, 278 (1959), 547-51
28. Thody, Philip (ed.), *Les Séquestrés d'Altona* (London: University of London Press, 1965)
29. ——, *Sartre* (London: Studio Vista, 1971)
30. Tynan, Kenneth: *Tynan Right and Left* (London: Longman, 1967)
31. Verstraeten, Pierre, *Violence et éthique* (Gallimard, 1972)
32. Williams, John, 'Sartre's Dialectic of History: *Les Séquestrés d'Altona*', *Renascence*, 22, 2 (1970), 59-68, 112

CRITICAL GUIDES TO FRENCH TEXTS

edited by
Roger Little, Wolfgang van Emden, David Williams

1. **David Bellos.** Balzac: La Cousine Bette.
2. **Rosemarie Jones.** Camus: L'Etranger *and* La Chute.
3. **W.D Redfern.** Queneau: Zazie dans le métro.
4. **R.C. Knight.** Corneille: Horace.
5. **Christopher Todd.** Voltaire: Dictionnaire philosophique.
6. **J.P. Little.** Beckett: En attendant Godot *and* Fin de partie.
7. **Donald Adamson.** Balzac: Illusions perdues.
8. **David Coward.** Duras: Moderato cantabile.
9. **Michael Tilby.** Gide: Les Faux-Monnayeurs.
10. **Vivienne Mylne.** Diderot: La Religieuse.
11. **Elizabeth Fallaize.** Malraux: La Voie Royale.
12. **H.T Barnwell.** Molière: Le Malade imaginaire.
13. **Graham E. Rodmell.** Marivaux: Le Jeu de l'amour et du hasard *and* Les Fausses Confidences.
14. **Keith Wren.** Hugo: Hernani *and* Ruy Blas.
15. **Peter S. Noble.** Beroul's Tristan *and the* Folie de Berne.
16. **Paula Clifford.** Marie de France: Lais.
17. **David Coward.** Marivaux: La Vie de Marianne *and* Le Paysan parvenu.
18. **J.H. Broome.** Molière: L'Ecole des femmes *and* Le Misanthrope.
19. **B.G. Garnham.** Robbe-Grillet: Les Gommes *and* Le Voyeur.
20. **J.P. Short.** Racine: Phèdre.
21. **Robert Niklaus.** Beaumarchais: Le Mariage de Figaro.
22. **Anthony Cheal Pugh.** Simon: Histoire.
23. **Lucie Polak.** Chrétien de Troyes: Cligés.
24. **John Cruickshank.** Pascal: Pensées.
25. **Ceri Crossley.** Musset: Lorenzaccio.
26. **J.W Scott.** Madame de Lafayette: La Princesse de Clèves.
27. **John Holyoake.** Montaigne: Essais.
28. **Peter Jimack.** Rousseau: Emile.
29. **Roger Little.** Rimbaud: Illuminations.

30. **Barbara Wright and David Scott.** Baudelaire: La Fanfarlo *and* Le Spleen de Paris.
31. **Haydn Mason.** Cyrano de Bergerac: L'Autre Monde.
32. **Glyn S. Burgess.** Chrétien de Troyes: Erec et Enide.
33. **S. Beynon John.** Anouilh: L'Alouette *and* Pauvre Bitos.
34. **Robin Buss.** Vigny: Chatterton.
35. **David Williams.** Rousseau: Les Rêveries du promeneur solitaire.
36. **Ronnie Butler.** Zola: La Terre.
37. **John Fox.** Villon: Poems.
38. **C.E.J. Dolamore.** Ionesco: Rhinocéros.
39. **Robert Lethbridge.** Maupassant: Pierre et Jean.
40. **David Curtis.** Descartes: Discours de la Méthode.
41. **Peter Cogman.** Hugo: Les Contemplations.
42. **Rosemary Lloyd.** Mallarmé: Poésies.
43. **M. Adereth.** Aragon: The Resistance Poems.
44. **Keith Wren.** Vigny: Les Destinées.
45. **Kathleen M. Hall and Margaret B. Wells.** Du Bellay: Poems.
46. **Geoffrey Bremner.** Diderot: Jacques le fataliste.
47. **Peter Dunwoodie.** Camus: L'Envers et l'Endroit *and* L'Exil et le Royaume.
48. **Michael Sheringham.** Beckett: Molloy.
49. **J.F. Falvey.** Diderot: Le Neveu de Rameau.
50. **Dennis Fletcher.** Voltaire: Lettres philosophiques.
51. **Philip Robinson.** Bernardin de Saint-Pierre: Paul et Virginie.
52. **Richard Griffiths.** Garnier: Les Juifves.
53. **Paula Clifford.** La Chastelaine de Vergi *and* Jean Renart: Le Lai de l'ombre.
54. **Robin Buss.** Cocteau: Les Enfants terribles.
55. **Tony Hunt.** Chrétien de Troyes: Yvain.
56. **Robert Gibson.** Alain-Fournier: Le Grand Meaulnes.
57. **James J. Supple.** Racine: Bérénice.
58. **Timothy Unwin.** Constant: Adolphe.
59. **David Shaw.** Molière: Les Précieuses ridicules.
60. **Roger Cardinal.** Breton: Nadja.

61. **Geoffrey N. Bromiley.** Thomas's Tristan *and the* Folie Tristan d'Oxford.
62. **R.J. Howells.** Rousseau: Julie ou la Nouvelle Héloïse.
63. **George Evans.** Lesage: Crispin rival de son maître *and* Turcaret.
64. **Paul Reed.** Sartre: La Nausée.
65. **Roger Mclure.** Sarraute: Le Planétarium.
66. **Denis Boak.** Sartre: Les Mots.
67. **Pamela M. Moores.** Vallès: L'Enfant.
68. **Simon Davies.** Laclos: Les Liaisons dangereuses.
69. **Keith Beaumont.** Jarry: Ubu Roi.
70. **G.J. Mallinson.** Molière: L'Avare.
71. **Susan Taylor-Horrex.** Verlaine: Fêtes galantes *and* Romances sans paroles.
72. **Malcolm Cook.** Lesage: Gil Blas.
73. **Sheila Bell.** Sarraute: Portrait d'un inconnu *and* Vous les entendez?
74. **W.D. Howarth.** Corneille: Le Cid.
75. **Peter Jimack.** Diderot: Supplément au Voyage de Bougainville.
76. **Christopher Lloyd.** Maupassant: Bel-Ami.
77. **David H. Walker.** Gide: Les Nourritures terrestres *and* La Symphonie pastorale
78. **Noël Peacock.** Molière: Les Femmes savantes.
79. **Jean H. Duffy.** Butor: La Modification.
80. **J.P. Little.** Genet: Les Nègres.
81. **John Campbell.** Racine: Britannicus.
82. **Malcolm Quainton.** D'Aubigné: Les Tragiques.
83. **Henry Phillips.** Racine: Mithridate.
84. **S. Beynon John.** Saint-Exupéry: Vol de Nuit *and* Terre des hommes.
85. **John Trethewey.** Corneille: L'Illusion comique *and* Le Menteur.
86. **John Dunkley.** Beaumarchais: Le Barbier de Séville.
87. **Valerie Minogue.** Zola: L'Assommoir.
88. **Kathleen Hall.** Rabelais: Pantagruel *and* Gargantua.

89. **A.W. Raitt.** Flaubert: Trois contes.
90. **Toby Garfitt.** Mauriac: Thérèse Desqueyroux.
91. **Margaret M. Callander.** Colette: Le Blé en herbe *and* La Chatte.
92. **David Whitton.** Molière: Le Bourgeois gentilhomme.
93. **Peter Cogman.** Mérimée: Colomba *and* Carmen.
94. **Derek A. Watts.** Corneille: Rodogune *and* Nicomède.
95. **Russell Cousins.** Zola: Thérèse Raquin.
96. **David Coward.** Pagnol: La Gloire de mon père *and* Le Château de ma mère.
97. **Kathleen M. McKilligan.** Mauriac: Le Nœud de vipères.
98. **Keith Busby.** Chrétien de Troyes: Perceval (Le Conte du Graal).
99. **Renate Günther.** Duras: Le Ravissement de Lol V. Stein *and* L'Amant.
100. **R.A. Francis.** Prévost: Manon Lescaut.
101. **John Fox.** The poetry of fifteenth-century France, 2 vols.
102. **J. Dryhurst.** Racine: Athalie.
103. **Ian R. Morrison.** Rabelais: Tiers Livre, Quart Livre, Ve Livre.
104. **Sara Poole.** Etcherelli: Elise ou la vraie vie.
105. **Christopher Betts.** Montesquieu: Lettres persanes.
106. **Richard Bolster.** Stendhal: Le Rouge et le Noir.
107. **Andrew Leak.** Barthes: Mythologies.